ISLAM
WORLD RELIGIONS

by Matthew S. Gordon

☑ Facts On File, Inc.

ISLAM, Revised Edition
World Religions

Facts On File, Inc.
132 West 31st Street
New York NY 10001

Gordon, Matthew.
Islam / by Matthew S. Gordon—Rev. ed.
        p. cm. — (World religions)
Includes bibliographical references and index.
Summary: An overview of Islam chronicling the religion's impact historically
and in the modern world and discussing its origins, basic beliefs, structure,
places of worship, and rites of passage.
        ISBN 0-8160-4401-5
        1. Islam. [1. Islam.] I. Title. II. Series.
BP161.2.G66 2001
297 — dc21   00-051858

Facts On File books are available at special discounts when purchased in bulk quantities
for businesses, associations, institutions, or sales promotions. Please call our Special
Sales Department in New York at 212/967-8800 or 800/322-8755.

You can find Facts On File on the World Wide Web at http://www.factsonfile.com

Developed by Brown Publishing Network, Inc.
Design Production by Jennifer Angell/Brown Publishing Network, Inc.
Photo Research by Nina Whitney
Photo credits:
Cover: Ascension of Mohammed, Iran, 1504. Giraudon/Art Resource, NY.
Title Page: Saudi Arabian boy at prayer, ARAMCO WORLD.
Table of Contents page: Mecca, midday prayer, AP/Wide World Photos.
Pages 6–7 UPI/Bettmann; 9 ARAMCO WORLD; 12-13 ARAMCO WORLD; 15 Christine Osborne
Pictures; 24 ARAMCO WORLD; 26 ARAMCO WORLD; 28–29 ARAMCO WORLD; 40 Art Resource,
NY; 43 The Bettmann Archive; 44-45 ARAMCO WORLD; 47 AP/Wide World Photos; 51 The
Bettmann Archive; 56 Christine Osborne Pictures; 58–59 Christine Osborn Pictures; 64
Christine Osborne Pictures; 67 Christine Osborne Pictures; 73 Art Resource, NY; 74-75 AP/
Wide World Photos; 77 Christine Osborne Pictures; 81 ARAMCO WORLD; 84 AP/Wide World
Photos; 88-89 UPI/Bettmann; 94 The Bettmann Archive; 99 Christine Osborne Pictures;
104–105 AP/Wide World Photos; 111 Christine Osborne Pictures; 114 UPI/Bettmann; 115 © Antoine
Gyori/CORBIS SYGMA; 121 ARAMCO WORLD; 123 Art Resource, NY.

Printed in the United States of America
RRD PKG 10 9 8 7 6 5 4 3 2
This book is printed on acid-free paper

TABLE OF CONTENTS

Preface   4

CHAPTER 1   Introduction: The Modern Islamic World   6

CHAPTER 2   Muhammad and the Founding of Islam   12

CHAPTER 3   The Spread of Islam   28

CHAPTER 4   Koran, Hadith and the Law   44

CHAPTER 5   The Variety of Religious Life in Islam   58

CHAPTER 6   Muslim Ritual Life   74

CHAPTER 7   The Patterns of Islamic Life   88

CHAPTER 8   Islam and the Modern World   104

               Glossary   124

               For Further Reading   126

               Index   127

Preface

The 20th century is sometimes called a "secular age," meaning, in effect, that religion is not an especially important issue for most people. But there is much evidence to suggest that this is not true. In many societies, including the United States, religion and religious values shape the lives of millions of individuals and play a key role in politics and culture as well.

The World Religions series, of which this book is a part, is designed to appeal to both students and general readers. The books offer clear, accessible overviews of the major religious traditions and institutions of our time. Each volume in the series describes where a particular religion is practiced, its origins and history, its central beliefs and important rituals, and its contributions to world civilization. Carefully chosen photographs complement the text, and a glossary and bibliography are included to help readers gain a more complete understanding of the subject at hand.

Religious institutions and spirituality have always played a central role in world history. These books will help clarify what religion is all about and reveal both the similarities and differences in the great spiritual traditions practiced around the world today.

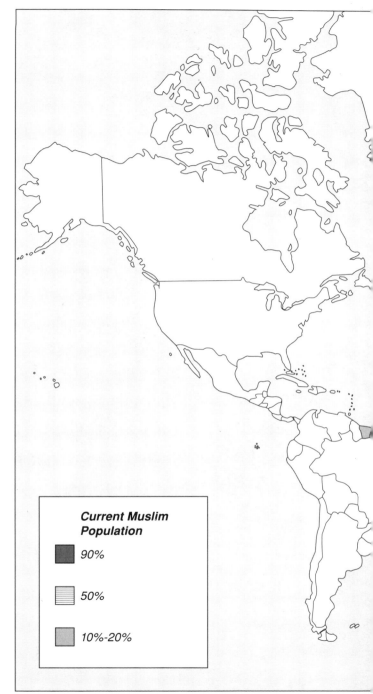

Current Muslim Population

90%

50%

10%-20%

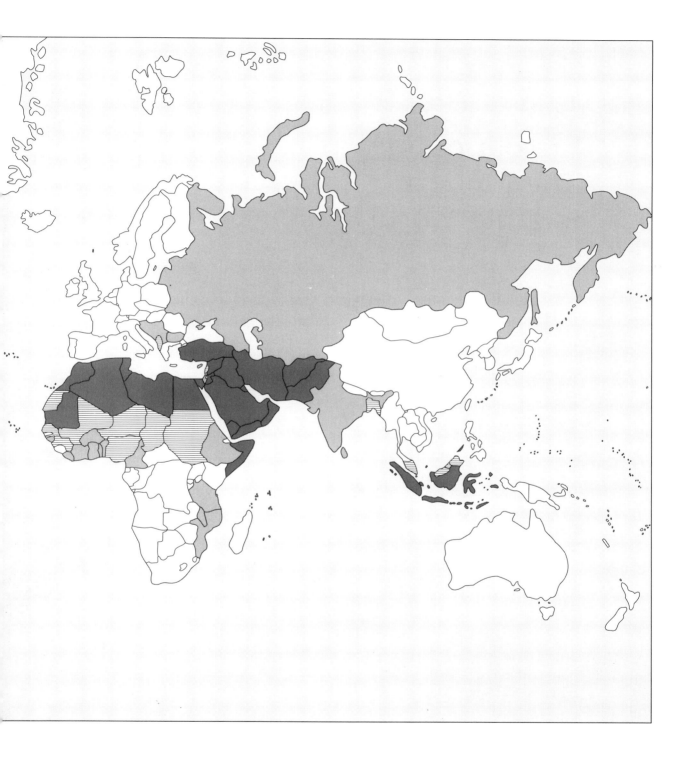

CHAPTER 1

Introduction:
The Modern
Islamic World

*I*slam, one of the most widespread religions in the world, is second only to Christianity in number of followers. The people who believe in the principles of Islam and practice its rituals are called Muslims, and they make up a large segment of the world population. Of the roughly six billion people in the world, over one billion are Muslims.

On the continents of Africa and Asia, and in the area known as the Middle East, Islam is the dominant religion in many countries, including Afghanistan, Algeria, Egypt, Iran, Iraq, Libya, Malaysia, Morocco, Saudi Arabia, and Syria. There are also Muslims in the states of the former Soviet Union, China, and Europe as well as on the continents of North and South America. The three countries with the largest Muslim communities are Indonesia, Pakistan, and Bangladesh—all in Asia.

Like the Jewish and Christian communities, the Islamic community comprises a number of small groups, among which beliefs differ slightly. There are, however, two overarching divisions within the faith: most Muslims belong to the Sunni sect and are known as Sunni Muslims; all other Muslims belong to the Shi'i

■ *Preceding page- An aerial view of the sacred mosque of Mecca. As the birthplace of the Prophet Muhammad, Mecca is one of the three holy cities for Muslims, Medina and Jerusalem being the other two. It was in Mecca, in the early 7th century, that Muhammad began to receive the divine revelation. Today, Mecca is a large, bustling city, quite unlike the small town into which the Prophet was born.*

sects and are known as the Shi'ah. The word "Shiite" is a variation of this term and one commonly used in the Western media. The largest group of Shi'ah are known as the Twelver Shi'ah. They form a majority in Iran and are represented by large communities in Iraq, Kuwait, Lebanon, and India. Several smaller branches of Shi'i Islam form communities in Yemen, India, and other countries as well.

Two Misconceptions about Islam

Despite its huge following around the world—and growing Muslim communities in the United States—Islam is foreign to most Americans, who are more familiar with Christianity or Judaism. Because most Americans know little or nothing about Islam, they have many misconceptions about Muslim beliefs and rituals. One common misconception is that all Muslims are Arabs. It is true that the Arabian Peninsula was the birthplace of Islam, that in the early years of Islam the majority of Muslims were Arabs, and that the holy text of Islam (the Koran) is written in the Arabic language. But only a century or so after the founding of Islam, the religion had spread to parts of southern Europe, east to Central Asia, India, and beyond. As it spread, Islam attracted growing numbers of converts among the peoples of these areas. Gradually the Arabs became but one in a variety of peoples that practiced the religion. As a result, most Muslims today are not Arabs. They do not speak Arabic, and the great majority live outside of the Middle East and North Africa—the two areas where the Arab population of the world is concentrated.

Another misconception is that the Muslim world is harsh and violent, and especially that it is hostile toward Westerners. This image is often presented in the European and North American media, which pay a great deal of attention to the activities of violent Muslim extremists. The World Trade Center bombing in New York City in 1993, the bombings of the United States Embassies in Kenya and Tanzania in 1998, and the harsh treatment of women in Afghanistan by the Taliban since 1994 are the kinds of events that receive extensive press coverage. The problem is that reporters often associate such things with Islam in a way that implies that all Muslims are violent—even that the

teachings of Islam advocate violence. In fact, the great majority of Muslims are peaceful, as their religion teaches them to be.

The negative image many people in the United Sates and Europe have of Islam and the Muslim world has a long history. In the Middle Ages, as the Christian Church and European royalty organized the Crusades against the Islamic world, the leaders of the church portrayed Muslims as barbaric and uncivilized. A few scholars and travelers from Europe and, later, the United States realized that these were ugly stereotypes and tried in vain to paint a more positive picture of Islam and the Muslims. Thus, the image of the barbaric Muslim has survived for generations and has spread throughout the Western world.

Stereotypes are false generalizations resulting from a lack of understanding. Many have judged Islam without making an effort to consider this religious tradition on its own terms, without bothering to become acquainted with its teaching and the ways

■ *Three generations of a Pakistani Muslim family. Dressed in the simple, white garment that symbolizes the purity and unity of their faith, they take part in the pilgrimage to Mecca, which is known as the Hajj. The pilgrimage brings together Muslims from all over the world, in particular, the continents of Asia and Africa.*

in which the Muslims practice their faith. The purpose of this book is to provide a better understanding of Islam so that the reader can begin to go beyond these stereotypes.

Islam: An Overview

Like Judaism and Christianity, Islam is a monotheistic religion—based on the belief in one God. Muslims use the Arabic word for God, *Allah*, to refer to the creator of the world and of all life within it. For Muslims, Allah is the lord of the universe.

The word "Islam" is Arabic and means submission to Allah. According to Islamic belief, God has sent a series of revelations down to human beings over the course of time. These include the revelations received by Moses and by the Christian prophet, Jesus. The Islamic tradition holds Moses and Jesus, as well as other prophets revered by the Jewish and Christian faiths, in great esteem. However, Muslims believe that these revelations, which came to humanity before the revelation of Islam, were corrupted—that human ideas and words were mixed with the divine message and that in their ignorance men and women neglected to follow God's teachings.

Muslims believe that God sent his message to humanity in order to guide those who were faithful to Him and to warn the evildoers of his anger. The man God chose to receive this new message was Muhammad ibn Abd Allah, a 40-year-old merchant of the Arabic town of Mecca. Sent to Muhammad in the middle of the 7th century, this revelation came to be known as the Koran. To the present day, the Koran remains for Muslims the literal Word of God. As the Koran itself says:

> *Allah, there is no god but He, the Living, the Self-subsistent.*
> *He has revealed to you the Book with the truth, confirming*
> *that which came before it. He also earlier revealed the Torah*
> *and the Gospel, as a source of guidance for people, and (now)*
> *He has sent down the Salvation.*

Ordered by God to spread the divine revelation, Muhammad slowly won over followers in Mecca and later in the nearby town of Medina. This was the first Islamic community and the seed from which would grow the modern Islamic world.

Muslims refer to their community as *ummah*, an Arabic word meaning community. For Muslims, ummah has a special connotation, however, because it occurs many times in the Koran. There, the term is used to mean religious community, including the religious communities of Jews and Christians and Muslims.

The foundation of the Islamic ummah is the collection of religious laws and duties known as the *Shari'ah*. The term is often translated as "holy law," but it is better thought of as the religious path Muslims are expected to follow. For devout Muslims, the Shari'ah is a set of regulations whose direct source is God; thus, to follow the Shari'ah is to follow and obey God's will.

However, the Shari'ah addresses more than matters of prayer and faith in God, which many people might think of as strictly religious concerns. It also deals with life in this world—how the community organizes its affairs and how members of the community live their lives. According to the Shari'ah, there is no real separation between religion and all other aspects of life. Therefore, devout Muslims seek to use the Shari'ah to guide them in every area of their day-to-day lives.

CHAPTER 2

Muhammad and the Founding of Islam

*T*he Islamic religion was born in the early 7th century in the city of Mecca, a small but bustling commercial center in the northwestern part of the Arabian Peninsula. Mecca's central market was usually crowded with flocks of sheep and goats, herds of camels, and the many townspeople and nomads who gathered there to buy and sell their wares. The sounds of haggling between the merchants and their clients rose and fell as the smells of spices, sheep pelts, fresh meat and dates mingled with the heat of the desert sun and the dust. This was the environment in which the prophet of Islam spent his early life, 1,400 years ago.

Muhammad ibn Abd Allah, born in Mecca around the year 570, was a member of the Banu Hashim, one of the town's Arab clans. His father died about the time of Muhammad's birth; his mother died when he was six. The orphan was then cared for by his grandfather, and upon the latter's death two years later, by his uncle Abu Talib. At the time, Abu Talib was the head of the Hashim clan. Poor and orphaned, Muhammad did not see much of a future ahead of him. Who could have guessed the course his life would take?

Arabia Prior to Islam

For most people who lived there, Arabia in the late 6th century was a difficult place in which to grow up. Most of the peninsula consisted on desert or arid steppe areas—an environment that demanded a great deal from even the strongest individuals. Only along the southern coastal areas, where higher elevations and sea breezes caused a milder climate, and along the far western mountainous region was nature less cruel.

In the wide stretches of desert, life centered on two kinds of communities. On a few oases and in small commercial centers, such as Mecca, people earned a living from agriculture and trading. The majority of the people who lived on the peninsula, however, were nomads who moved each year with their belongings and animals from one grazing area to the next. In both the sedentary and nomadic communities, society was organized around clans. These, in turn, made up larger tribes.

The tribe was the cornerstone of society in early Arabia. It provided its members with support, protection against enemies, and a sense of identity. Belonging to a powerful tribe that could always protect its members was obviously advantageous.

The tribal leaders, known as *shaykhs*, usually came from the larger, wealthier clans of each tribe; they made most of the decisions affecting the tribe. Poorer, smaller clans had to abide by the decisions of the larger ones and often resented doing so.

The nomadic tribes got milk and fresh meat from their flocks and herds as well as the wool and camel hair they needed for clothing, blankets, and material for tents. Because most tribes were poor and had few possessions apart from their animals, they sometimes raided others for whatever they could carry away.

The purpose of the raid, or *ghazwah*, was seldom to kill one's enemies. Rather, it was to steal animals, goods, and when possible, women from the opposing tribe. The animals and goods added to the meager wealth of the tribe; the women were either kept or sold as slaves. The raid was also a time for tribes to demonstrate their strength, and for the individual members of the tribe, their courage.

Although killing the members of opposing tribes was not usually the goal of a raid, it was often unavoidable. Arabia, prior

to the coming of Islam, had no central government; tribes took it upon themselves to avenge the wrongs done to one of their number. As a result, vengeance killings were common among nomadic tribes. On occasion, these acts of revenge led to costly feuds between tribes. While many decried the costs of these feuds, there was little anyone could do to prevent them.

Leading a tribe was consequently no easy task. In an environment where threats from nature and from other tribes were constant, only the most practical and courageous could succeed in positions of leadership. Those who displayed such qualities were highly respected by all. Only one other voice in the community was listened to as closely as the shaykh's—that of the poet.

■ Arab nomads in an area of the Syrian desert. In the 7th century, during the Prophet's lifetime, nomadism was a common way of life in many parts of the Middle East including the Arabian Peninsula. Over the course of this century, nomadism has slowly disappeared, in part because many nomadic groups either choose or are forced to settle down, and must seek other forms of livelihood.

For the Arabs of this period, there was no higher form of expression than poetry. But the poet was more than a valued member of society who sang of the joys and hardships of life. Poets, especially those who demonstrated great eloquence, were believed to be possessed by *jinn*—the spirits that inhabited the natural world. Thus it was thought that poets had supernatural powers with which they could defeat enemies; and frequently poets were called on to use these powers.

In this harsh environment, many people looked to religion for comfort. Although Christianity and Judaism had made inroads into the peninsula by the time of Muhammad's birth, most people practiced forms of religion that were native to their area. They believed, for example, that the jinn could work evil or good, and it was important never to anger them. Consequently, in certain areas such as sites believed to be the burial place of a spirit, mounds of stones were erected, and offerings, sometimes of food, were left beside these stone markers to please the jinn.

Some of the early Arabs also revered certain gods and goddesses. Although these divinities varied according to the tribe or area of the peninsula, there seems to have been a common belief in at least one of these gods: Allah, the creator of the universe. Allah was probably considered the supreme god, but, unlike the other deities beneath him, he was thought to have little involvement in the daily lives of people.

The Town of Mecca

In Mecca and the surrounding region, known as the Hijaz, the most popular deities were three goddesses said to be the daughters of Allah. Idols were dedicated to them, and often, the surrounding area was considered sacred, within which no animal could be killed and in which tribesmen in trouble—for whatever reason—could claim refuge.

At the time of Muhammad's birth, Mecca was an important religious center for the tribes of western and central Arabia. Its sanctuary dedicated to the three principal goddesses was located in an area known as the Ka'bah which held idols representing these and other gods and goddesses. The area had been built around a mysterious black stone, perhaps a meteorite, that was venerated by the tribes of the area. Each year, local tribesmen visited Mecca to see the Ka'bah. The pilgrimage, known as the *hajj*, included a ceremonial procession around the sacred shrine.

Mecca was, therefore, not only a commercial but also a religious center. Pilgrims came to worship at the Ka'bah, and, because it was a sacred shrine around which violence was prohibited, many also came to buy and sell their goods. Those who benefitted the most from this activity were the merchant families of Mecca.

By the time of Muhammad's birth, the leaders of these families had come to dominate Meccan society because they controlled the flow of goods in and out of the town. They were business people who recognized that much of the commerce within the town depended upon the pilgrims. To assure that the pilgrimage ran smoothly, these families took control of the sanctuary of the Ka'bah. As a result, they virtually controlled life in Mecca and the surrounding areas. For these large clans, it was a time of prosperity and political strength.

Although these groups certainly benefited from Mecca's prosperity, many other people of the area did not. With the growing commerce had come new sets of values and concerns. Where once the tribe and the health of the community were given priority, now materialism and a new concern with individual wealth and power undermined traditional values. Increasingly the larger clans dominated the smaller, poorer ones, denying them a share in the town's growing wealth. As values changed and the gap between rich and poor widened, resentment among the less fortunate began to intensify.

It was an uneasy world into which Muhammad was born. The shift from communal values to a more individualistic way of life caused many to ask difficult questions about the world around them. These questions were less about money and power and more about the meaning of the world and individual destiny. Traditional practices no longer provided the answers these people were seeking. For many it was a time of spiritual uneasiness.

Some may have converted to Christianity or to Judaism, which had spread to the Arabian Peninsula. Jewish tribes had lived in the town of Yathrib—a prosperous agricultural center not far from Mecca—for generations and were a well-established part of the community. Although no Christian tribes inhabited Arabia at the time, there were numerous Christian Arabs in areas north of the peninsula. These groups, which comprised various Christian sects, were ruled by the Byzantine Empire, the capital of which was Constantinople (known today as Istanbul, the capital of Turkey). The merchants of Mecca no doubt traded with these Christians regularly.

Muhammad's Early Life

Little is known about the Meccans who converted to Christianity and Judaism, but it is reasonably certain that as the Meccans had increasing contact with the rest of Arabia and with the areas beyond its borders, they became acquainted with Jewish and Christian beliefs and practices. For those Meccans haunted by questions of individual destiny, such religious beliefs must have seemed attractive.

In Mecca itself, however, neither Christianity nor Judaism had much of a presence. The powerful merchant clans remained in control of religious life in the town and were presumably careful not to allow new practices and beliefs to cross the borders. Meccans who did not travel therefore sought new beliefs within Mecca itself. The orphan Muhammad was soon to fulfill this need.

Little is known about Muhammad's early life. His uncle Abu Talib provided him with clothing and a home, but never taught him to read or write. Later in his life he depended on his followers to write down the words of the revelation in order to preserve them. It is believed that in his teens Muhammad worked as a camel driver, accompanying his uncle and other merchants on their travels into southern Syria and on the peninsula itself. In this way, Muhammad gained exposure to places outside of Mecca and grew familiar with their different customs. For the most part the Meccans traded with other Arab tribes and the settled Arabic-speaking population of Syria. Because these included Christian communities, Muhammad came in contact with this monotheistic tradition. How much he actually learned about Christian beliefs remains uncertain.

In the year 595, Muhammad's life took a dramatic turn. For a time he had been working for an older merchant—a wealthy woman named Khadijah. He had shown himself to be intelligent and responsible, impressing her so much that she proposed marriage. He accepted and thus became a successful member of the Meccan merchant class. During the next 15 years, Muhammad enjoyed a life of prosperity. As a merchant, he continued to travel to other areas of the peninsula and farther north, encountering the ideas and practices of Jewish and Christian communities. Again, it is hard to tell what he learned about these beliefs.

Unlike other merchants, Muhammad found only passing satisfaction with the comforts such a life provided. He seems to have been aware of the decline in traditional values within Meccan society and of the unhappiness felt by many in the area. Having known poverty as a young boy, Muhammad was sensitive to the grievances of the less fortunate. He began to question the direction that both his life and that of his community was taking.

The Coming of Revelation

By the age of 40, Muhammad had begun to spend time alone, meditating on the questions that troubled him. On occasion he would spend nights in a small cave near Mecca. It was common for men to go on retreat, so few thought his behavior odd. During one such night Muhammad experienced what he thought were strange visions. As Muslims are taught, the angel Gabriel appeared before him in human form. Seizing hold of Muhammad, the angel ordered him to recite a short set of words. When he did so, the angel released him.

Convinced that he was either losing his mind or that spirits had possessed him, Muhammad fled from the cave. Partly down the hill he heard a voice behind him say: "Oh, Muhammad, you are the Messenger of God, and I am Gabriel."

Confused and terrified, Muhammad was convinced his sanity had left him. Only as the experiences continued—and with the encouragement of Khadijah, who was sure the words came from God—did Muhammad come to believe that the words he was asked to recite were revelations from God and that God now expected him to serve as his divine messenger.

Overwhelmed at first, Muhammad told only Khadijah and a few close followers. Slowly he began to preach more openly to the

Meccan community. As the biographers of Muhammad tell us, Muhammad continued to receive revelations for the next 20 years, and until the end of his life he passed them on to his followers. This is why Muslims call Muhammad the Messenger of God.

It took Muhammad several years to overcome his initial doubts and to realize the importance of his task. But by 613, he was convinced that he was meant to follow in the footsteps of the prophets before him—Abraham, Moses and Jesus, among others—and to bring God's word to mankind. As a result, Muhammad assumed the title of Prophet of God and began to preach openly in the streets.

At first, Muhammad's message was a simple one: He declared that there was only one god, Allah, and that there was nothing like him. Like the prophets before him, Muhammad also preached of the power of God and the certainty that the day of judgment was to come.

At first, Muhammad's preaching was ignored by the leaders of Mecca. They had heard similar ideas from Jews and Christians, so they assumed that Muhammad was only repeating those ideas. Before long, however, the Meccans began to realize the meaning of Muhammad's teachings. For instance, Muhammad called on people to worship only Allah and to reject the cult of the goddesses. He stressed that to worship any other deity—whether goddess, idol or jinn—was to violate the absolute oneness of God.

These teachings challenged the entire system upon which Meccan leaders had established their power and wealth. Realizing that if Muhammad succeeded in convincing people of the truth of his message, that structure would collapse, they were determined to see that Muhammad failed.

The Opposition to Muhammad

As the top Meccan families turned against Muhammad, using threats and insults as well as physical violence, Muhammad realized that he and his followers must leave Mecca. In the year 619, they moved to nearby Ta'if for refuge, but the main tribe of Ta'if, the Banu Thaqif, refused to let them remain, and they were obliged to make their way back to Mecca.

This was only one in a series of setbacks for Muhammad in 619. Two of his most loyal supporters had passed away earlier that year: his beloved wife, Khadijah, and his uncle Abu Talib. With the death of Abu Talib, who had protected the Muslims, Muhammad lost an important friend.

However, the year 619 was marked not only by sadness; it was also the year in which, according to the Islamic tradition, Muhammad experienced one of the most remarkable events of his life. Asleep one night near the Ka'bah, Muhammad was woken by the angel Gabriel. With Gabriel as his guide, Muhammad journeyed to Jerusalem, then, from a prominent rock, to heaven. There he is said to have met with the great prophets Abraham, Jesus, Moses and others. At the climax of his journey, he is believed to have stood before God. For Muslims, this miraculous journey is further evidence of Muhammad's profound spiritual nature.

Muhammad still faced the hostility of the Meccans. It became essential that he find a place outside Mecca that would welcome him and his followers. The solution came in the year 620. Among the pilgrims who visited Mecca that year was a group of men from the northern town of Yathrib (also known as Medina). The men had heard of Muhammad and were impressed with his teachings. In their first meeting with him, they told him of the problems facing their town. Rival tribes had taken up arms in a bloody feud, and chaos threatened the town. Having failed to find a solution, the men had come seeking an outsider who could restore peace.

Over the next two years, the men returned with others from Medina, and a group of them converted to Islam. Encouraged by this new support, Muhammad urged his Meccan followers to make their way to Medina, where they could begin a new life as Muslims. Gradually, they left Mecca and traveled north to what would become their home for roughly the next decade.

When Muhammad received word that a group of Meccans were planning to kill him, he arranged to leave Mecca that very night—in late September 622 Muhammad and his closest adviser, Abu Bakr, made their way to a cave outside the town. There they hid from the assassins for three days. According to legend the mouth of the cave was covered by the web of a spider moments before the Meccans rode by. One of the men glanced down from his horse, saw the delicate web covering the entrance and remarked that surely no one could be inside the cave.

With the way clear, Muhammad and Abu Bakr traveled to Medina, where they were greeted joyfully by the waiting Muslims and their Medinan supporters. This journey, from Mecca to Medina, is one of the key events of Muhammad's life. It signalled not only his escape to safety, but, far more importantly, the establishment of the Islamic community. The journey is known to Muslims as the Hijrah, and the event came to be recognized as marking the beginning of the Islamic calendar.

Muhammad: Politics and Prophethood

The community of Muslims that welcomed Muhammad to Medina was made up of both Meccans and Medinans. Muhammad knew that he had to avoid showing favoritism to either group. In one of his first decisions as leader of this community, he demonstrated his political skills. Faced with offers from both groups to make his home with them, he wisely avoided the decision. He simply let his camel roam free, and at the spot where the animal came to rest, Muhammad established his home. Several huts were erected for Muhammad and the two women he had married since the death of Khadijah in 619. Beside these, a large space was cleared and a rough structure built. This was the first mosque built in Medina. Muhammad was now set to continue his divinely appointed task.

Muhammad's responsibilities in Medina were daunting. Not only did he continue receiving revelations from God and teaching his followers, but he was now also the leader of the young Muslim community. He faced a host of problems: he had to find a solution to the feuds that were dividing the town; he had to find work and shelter for the Meccans who had come to Medina with him; he had to counter opposition to the teachings of Islam within Medina; and he still faced the challenge of the Meccan merchant clans that were determined to see him and his community destroyed.

In solving the problems between the Medinans, Muhammad convinced the feuding clans that they should join the community of Muslims. He worked out a series of agreements that forged strong links between the Meccans and those Medinans who accepted his teachings. He faced, however, mounting distrust from one group in Medina—the Jewish tribes.

Three tribes made up the Jewish population of Medina. At first, they had welcomed Muhammad because of the peace he promised to bring. Soon, however, they began to have second thoughts about his leadership and his teachings. Initially Muhammad considered incorporating certain Jewish practices into the rituals of Islam, and for a time, Muslims and Jews prayed together in the direction of Jerusalem. Then, in the year 624, Muhammad received inspiration from God to instruct his followers to pray in the direction of Mecca. This caused a break with the Jewish tribes. From that point forward relations between the Jews of Medina and the Muslim community worsened and ended finally in violence. Two of the Jewish tribes were driven from Medina, while the male members of the third tribe suffered execution at the hands of the Muslims.

Muhammad turned his attention to the problem of providing for those of his followers who had come with him from Mecca. Medina was an agricultural town, but the Meccan Muslims lacked experience in farming. Instead of having them learn to farm, Muhammad decided to have them engage in a more familiar activity—raiding. Arming his male followers, Muhammad sent them against the trade caravans that crossed the peninsula. A series of raids were carried out successfully, and in this way the Muslim community was able to provide for its needs.

The Clash of Arms

The Meccans were outraged. They depended on the caravan trade for their livelihood and viewed these attacks as an attempt by Muhammad to undermine their power. Their opportunity to respond to the Muslims came in the year 624. A large caravan was reported to be on its way to Mecca from the north. Expecting the Muslims to launch a raid, the Meccans sent a strong force to escort the caravan into the area.

Muhammad had indeed sent a group of Muslim raiders against the caravan. At a place named Badr the two small forces clashed. Although the Muslims were outnumbered 3-to-1, they

fought bravely and finally routed the Meccan fighters. This victory was seen by the Muslims as proof of divine guidance, and that they were indeed chosen by God for a special purpose.

The following year, the Meccan leadership set out to avenge the loss at Badr. Organizing a huge force , they set out against Muhammad and his people. The two armies met near the mountain of Uhud, and this time the Muslims met with defeat, losing both dead and wounded to the Meccans. This came as a blow to the Muslims, some of whom questioned whether God was really behind Muhammad and his community. The debate was settled when a revelation came to Muhammad in which the defeat was represented as a test for the true believer. Those who held firmly to their beliefs would find reward from God.

Despite their victory, the Meccans returned to Mecca, leaving the Muslims a chance to regroup. The following year, the

Muslims faced perhaps their greatest challenge from Mecca. In an effort to crush the Muslim community, the Meccans organized a huge force and marched directly on Medina. Following the advice of one of his followers, Muhammad had a long trench dug in front of Medina. The trench prevented the Meccans from riding up to the town. After a time, the Meccan forces grew restless, many of the nomads in the army left and the campaign was called off. Although little fighting had taken place, the Muslims viewed the event as a victory—and further proof that God was on their side.

Following this battle, Muhammad turned against the last of the Jewish tribes. The tribe had negotiated with the Meccans and so was accused by the Muslims of treachery. After surrendering to Muhammad's forces, the men of the tribe were put to the sword, and the women and children sold into slavery. This brought to an end all opposition to Muhammad within Medina. Muhammad now resumed his efforts to defeat his sworn enemies—the leaders of Mecca.

In the hope of settling matters without further bloodshed, Muhammad announced that he and a group of Muslims would go to Mecca to perform the traditional ceremonies at the Ka'bah. When they reached Mecca, however, they were met by an armed force. Muhammad insisted his intentions were peaceful, but the Meccan forces would not budge. After heated negotiations, the Muslims agreed to leave and not return until the following year, when they would enter the city to perform the ceremonies. While many Muslims were disappointed with the decision not to attack Mecca, Muhammad told them that the agreement represented recognition from the Meccans of Muhammad's leadership and of the strength of the Muslim community—and thus it was a victory for them and for Islam.

Having set aside the issue of the Meccans for the moment, Muhammad sought to subdue those tribes of the region that had supported his enemies. He marched on the town of Khaybar, which his forces took after a prolonged siege. Then the Muslims moved steadily against other tribes that had allied with their enemies. One by one they defeated these tribes and made them swear allegiance to Islam. With these victories, Muhammad's hold over the peninsula was secure.

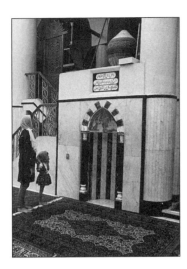

*Two young Muslims visit the Prophet's Mosque in Medina. They stand in front of the **mihrab**, a small niche located in all mosques which indicates the propper direction of prayer. Muslims must pray in the direction of Mecca, the site of the holy Ka'ba. Medina is located three hundred miles north of Mecca, and during the annual Hajj, many pilgrims travel to Medina to visit the mosque and the Prophet's tomb.*

The following year the Meccans opened their town to the Muslims, who peacefully carried out the ceremonies under the leadership of Muhammad. The next year, however, tensions reemerged, and Muhammad decided to use force against the Meccans. With his army, Muhammad marched on Mecca ready for battle. As he approached the city, however, he was met by the head of the Meccans, Abu Sufyan, who had decided that Mecca could no longer resist the Muslims. Abu Sufyan surrendered the town and the sacred sanctuary to Muhammad.

Entering the town, Muhammad proceeded directly to the Ka'bah. Placing his hand upon the black stone, he shouted in a clear voice "Allahu Akbar" (God is most great). With this, Muhammad was affirming the most basic of Islamic beliefs—the supreme oneness of God. He then ordered that the idols of the Ka'bah be destroyed. This brought an end to the cult of the goddesses and the use of the Ka'bah as a shrine of this cult. The Ka'bah, from that moment on, was claimed by the Muslims as the central sanctuary of the Islamic religion, a status it retains to the present day.

Victory and the Final Pilgrimage

The year was 630, and Muhammad stayed for only a short time in Mecca—long enough to establish Muslim control over the town and to win the support of the Meccan population. For the next two years, Muhammad expanded his influence throughout the Arabian Peninsula. He sent envoys to distant tribes, calling on them to convert to Islam. Many of the tribes did so with little protest, whereas others were convinced only with the use of force. Before long, Muhammad controlled most of the peninsula.

In the year 632, Muhammad again set out for Mecca to perform the annual pilgrimage to the Ka'bah. In previous years, Muhammad had permitted both Muslims and non-Muslims to carry out the pilgrimage. This year, however, he ruled that now only Muslims could worship at the Ka'bah. From that time forward, the rituals and the sacred sanctuary were to be dedicated solely to the worship of Allah.

On the 10th day of the pilgrimage, after the required rituals, Muhammad spoke to the Muslims in his last great sermon. He spoke to them of their obligations as members of the community of Muslims, and he urged them to treat each other well and thus maintain the unity of Islam. He ended the sermon with this reminder: "I have left amongst you that which, if you hold fast to it, shall preserve you from all error, a clear indication, the Book of God, and the word of His Prophet. O, people, hear my words and understand."

He then recited to them the final revelation, one it is believed he had received from God only a short time earlier:

> *Today the unbelievers have despaired of your religion;*
> *therefore fear them not, but fear you Me.*
> *Today I have perfected your religion for you,*
> *and I have completed My blessing upon you,*
> *and I have approved Islam for your religion.* (5.3)

With the pilgrimage complete, Muhammad left for Medina. Known as the Farewell Pilgrimage, this was to be the last time Muhammad would see Mecca. Not long after his return to Medina, Muhammad fell ill, and late on the 12th day of Rabi I, the third month of the Islamic calendar, he died.

The Islamic community now faced a troubling question: Who was to lead the community now that Muhammad was gone? In bringing the Koran to mankind, he had fulfilled his tasks as the messenger of God. However, he had also founded a community that had come to depend upon his leadership and teachings. After Muhammad's death, it was up to the community to find a successor.

CHAPTER 3

The Spread
of Islam

M|uhammad had not left instructions on how to choose a successor. The Muslims themselves had to resolve this problem as best they could.

On the evening of Muhammad's death, a group of Muslims debated the issue. Finally, they selected Abu Bakr as their new leader. He had been one of the first Meccans to convert to Islam and had consistently shown his loyalty to Muhammad. The decision was approved by the community, and Abu Bakr was given the title of *caliph*, or successor, which meant that he took over Muhammad's role as the political leader of the Islamic community. The state that he and those who ruled after him would run would be called the *caliphate*.

The First Three Caliphs and the Early Conquests

Under the leadership of Abu Bakr, an important step was taken by the Islamic community: the final conquest of the Arabian Peninsula. During Muhammad's lifetime, most of the Arab tribes in Arabia had agreed to accept the teachings of Islam. Following his death, however, many broke away. Abu Bakr sent forces to

bring these tribes back under the rule of Islam. Within a short time, the entire peninsula fell under Muslim control.

The decision to send forces beyond the limits of the Arabian Peninsula had been made earlier by Muhammad. Since he died before carrying out these plans, it was up to Abu Bakr and his successors to do so.

The Middle East was then controlled by two rival empires. In the areas of what we call today Syria, Egypt and Turkey, the Byzantine Empire held sway. Further to the east, in Iraq and Iran, was the empire of the Sasanians. For decades conflict between the two empires had weakened them both politically and economically. Neither empire was prepared to meet the unexpected threat from the Arabian Peninsula to the south.

Although Abu Bakr organized the first attacks against Syria and Iraq, he died shortly after the fighting began, in 634. The position of caliph then passed to Umar ibn al-Khattab. Umar, who would rule over the Muslims for about a decade, proved to be an excellent choice.

Skilled in both politics and military strategy, Umar is considered one of the greatest figures of early Islamic history because under his leadership the Islamic empire flourished and spread. He sent his armies deep into Syria, where they defeated the forces of the Byzantine Empire. They captured Damascus and Jerusalem, then moved against Egypt, where, once again, Byzantine forces were defeated and sent into full retreat north.

Meanwhile, Muslim armies battled the Persian Sasanid dynasty in Iraq and Iran. In several battles, the Muslims inflicted heavy losses on the Persian troops. Although Umar would not live to see the final collapse of the Sasanid Empire, by the end of his life all of Iraq and a large piece of Iran had fallen into Muslim hands.

With Umar's death in 644, a new caliph was chosen for the growing empire. He was Uthman ibn Affan, a merchant from the Umayyad family. This family had been opposed to Muhammad when he began his preaching in Mecca and after his move to Medina. Although the family finally converted to Islam, there were still bad feelings between the Umayyads and other groups within the Islamic community. During Uthman's caliphate, these feelings deepened until many Muslims began to oppose Uthman.

Under Uthman, Muslim forces continued to conquer new areas: From Egypt, they pushed west into North Africa, and in Iran they continued to defeat the Sasanians. Soon, however, the Muslims were forced to turn their attention to the increasing tension between Uthman and various groups within the community.

For the First Time, Muslim against Muslim

Tensions finally exploded in the year 656 with the assassination of Uthman. Although a new caliph was quickly chosen, Uthman's murder sent shock waves throughout the community and led to civil war. For the first time, Muslims were armed against each other. The man chosen to succeed Uthman was Ali ibn Abi Talib, the son-in-law and cousin of Muhammad and one of his earliest converts. While highly respected for his close relationship with Muhammad and for his service to Islam, Ali soon found himself in serious trouble.

Uthman's family, the Umayyads, was now led by Mu'awiyah, who was then the Muslim governor of Syria. He was sharply critical of Ali for not having done enough to punish Uthman's killers. When Ali tried to make Mu'awiyah step down as governor, Mu'awiyah refused; Ali felt obliged to send an army against him. At first, Ali's troops did well against the Syrian forces. Desperate, Mu'awiyah was able to convince Ali to open negotiations. Ali agreed and the fighting was stopped. It was a decision that Ali was soon to regret.

The core of Ali's army was made up of his closest followers. When Ali opened talks with the Syrians, a group of these followers broke with him, saying that he did not have the right to halt the fighting. Fiercely devout Muslims, they argued that only God had the power to make such a decision. In their view, the only person with the right to rule the community was the successor to Muhammad, who was now Ali; anyone who challenged the ruler was standing against the community and, worse, against the will of God. They argued that because Ali had not defended the community by defeating Mu'awiyah, he had gone against God and, therefore, was no longer worthy of being ruler.

This group, known as the Kharijites, now took up arms against the community. Ali, as ruler, had little choice but to send troops against his former followers. In several clashes, he was able to subdue the Kharijites. He was not able to crush the movement completely, however, and in 662 a Kharijite stabbed Ali to death.

Civil strife had created deep divisions within the Islamic community, and it was not clear who would rule. Into this vacuum stepped Mu'awiyah, who was still governor of Syria and head of a powerful army. Claiming the title of caliph for himself, Mu'awiyah moved the capital of the empire from Medina to Damascus. Although many opposed this decision, no other group could challenge Mu'awiyah.

The Umayyads and the Shi'ah

The move to Damascus brought an end to the first period of Islamic history. What had once been a small community of Muslims, centered around Muhammad, had become a powerful empire in control of a large part of the Middle East and North Africa. A new dynasty, the Umayyads, was now in control of the caliphate, and it faced all the problems that come with trying to run a huge empire.

Among these problems was the opposition of the Kharijites. Although they had been defeated by Ali, the Kharijites continued to attract followers with their radical message that the Umayyads had seized power against the will of God. Branding these rulers as illegitimate, they called for Muslims to rise up against the dynasty. In response, the Umayyads sent a series of forces against the Kharijites but with mixed results. Although they defeated the radicals in battle, they could not squash the spread of Kharijite ideas.

The Umayyads faced opposition from another group as well: the followers of Ali ibn Abi Talib and his family. As an early convert to Islam Ali had attracted an intensely loyal group of followers known as the Shi'at Ali, or the Followers of Ali. These Shi'ah, as they came to be known, fought with Ali against Mu'awiyah and the Umayyads. Although Ali's assassination shook them deeply, they remained loyal to both his name and his family.

The Shi'ah believed that when Muhammad died he had intended for Ali to succeed him as leader of the community. They argued that Muhammad had given a sermon in which he said that after he was gone the Muslims should follow Ali. For this reason, when Abu Bakr, Umar and Uthman were chosen as the next caliphs, the Shi'ah protested, saying that only Ali and his family had the right to lead the community after Muhammad. The Shi'ah would remain from this time forward a minority Islamic sect— often persecuted by the majority of Muslims, who belonged to the Sunni branch of Islam and found that sect's beliefs unacceptable.

After Ali's death, the Shi'ah turned their attention to Ali's son, Hasan. At the time, Hasan was a religious scholar in the town of Medina and had stayed clear of politics, to the disappointment of the Shi'ah, until his death in 669. The loyalties of the Shi'ah then shifted to his brother, the famous Husayn.

Husayn was cut from different cloth than his brother. Although cautious, he was also very proud of his family's name. When the Shi'ah urged him to claim his right to the caliphate in the year 680, Husayn agreed to try. Only a short time before, news had come of the death of Mu'awiyah. Mu'awiyah's son Yazid had taken over, but the Shi'ah felt that the time was ripe for revolt. Their center of activity was the city of Kufah. They sent messengers to Husayn in Medina, urging him to come to Kufah to lead them against the hated Umayyads.

Husayn decided to take his chances. He set out for Kufah with his family and a small band of followers. The Umayyad caliph, Yazid, hearing news of Husayn's march, immediately sent troops to prevent the group from reaching Kufah. Near the town of Karbala, tragedy struck. Husayn and his small group were attacked by the Umayyad troops. One by one, Husayn's followers fell, followed finally by Husayn himself. It is said that the soldiers hesitated before dealing the final blow to the grandson of the Prophet.

Husayn is said then to have been beheaded by one of the soldiers. His head was sent to the caliph Yazid in Damascus. Yazid gloated over the head, and made crude remarks about Husayn and the rest of Ali's family. For his role in Husayn's death, Yazid would never be forgiven by the Shi'ah.

These events, which occured during the month of Muharram, were felt deeply by the Shi'ah. They had placed great hopes in Husayn, and so his death cast a pall over their community. Mixed with this sadness was guilt because they had failed to come to Husayn's assistance when he needed them. Since that time, the Shi'ah remember Husayn's sacrifice through special rituals and prayers held every year during the month of Muharram, the first Islamic month.

The killing of Husayn did not bring an end to the activities of the Shi'ah, many of whom began looking to other members of Ali's family to lead them. During the next few decades, these men would lead revolts against the Umayyads but with no success. For the Umayyads, the Shi'ah remained a thorny problem.

The Umayyads and New Conquests

Although the Umayyads were eventually overthrown, the Shi'ah continued to see them as the symbol of unjust government. Even today, when the Shi'ah criticize modern political leaders, they often compare them to the Umayyads of the 7th century.

The Umayyad dynasty lasted for roughly a hundred years during which the Islamic Empire grew in both size and power. Umayyad forces extended the rule of Islam west across North Africa to the Atlantic coast. Turning north, the Muslim armies crossed the Straits of Gibraltar and invaded Spain. They moved swiftly across Spain and into southern France. Only in the year 732 were they finally halted by a Frankish army under the command of Charles Martel. Despite this defeat, Spain remained in Muslim hands. For the next 750 years, Spain would be a dynamic Islamic land.

The Umayyad armies continued to drive eastward. The remaining areas of Iran fell to the Muslims as did Afghanistan and the area we now call Pakistan. With these new possessions, the empire reached new levels of power. Much of the wealth of the Umayyad caliphate came from the taxes that the caliphs imposed on the peoples conquered over the years.

For all their authority, the Umayyads still faced serious political problems. The Kharijites and the Shi'ah were still active, and both groups—especially the Shi'ah—spread propaganda against the Umayyads. On occasion, one or the other of the two movements would organize a bloody revolt. Nor were these the only groups opposed to the Umayyads; many other Muslims were angry with the ruling dynasty. One common complaint was that wealth and privileges were not fairly distributed by the Umayyads and their supporters.

These feelings of frustration helped fuel a revolutionary movement that had secretly been forming in the eastern province of Khurasan, which is today part of Central Asia. By the year 750, the Umayyad family was on the defensive, and much of the empire had fallen into the hands of the revolutionaries, who at that point selected a new caliph for the empire: Abu al-Abbas. He was a member of the Abbasid family and ruled only for a short time before his brother, al-Mansur, came to power. Al-Mansur ruled for many years.

The Abbasid Caliphate

The Abbasids ruled from 750 to 1258. In the first 200 years of their rule, they reached dizzying heights of power and wealth. Their empire stretched from Morocco to India, and the Abbasid caliphs earned the respect of the entire world. Their wealth came from many sources. With their army and navy, the caliphs controlled the trade routes that crisscrossed the empire. Their empire produced vast amounts of agricultural products and took in revenue through taxation, allowing the early Abbasids to live in great splendor.

To run their empire, the Abbasids developed a large bureaucratic government centered in Baghdad. Soon this new capital became a major urban center—the hub of political and economic activity for the whole empire. To defend themselves and the empire, they established a powerful standing army based in garrisons throughout the Islamic lands. An impressive intelligence network backed the army with informants who worked in every corner of the empire. The most important army was kept in Baghdad, where it could defend the ruling family and the state.

Under these early Abbasid caliphs, the Islamic community experienced a period of cultural brilliance. In Baghdad and other cities, the caliphs used their influence to encourage poets, writers and musicians. Many great works were created in this period as a result, including the famous *Arabian Nights* (also known as *One*

Thousand and One Nights). The Abbasids also commissioned architects and builders to construct palaces and magnificent homes in the capital and other regions. For a short period, the capital was moved to the city of Samarra, also on the Euphrates, where the ruins of the many palaces built by this dynasty are still visible.

The Abbasids also provided a great deal of support to the scholarly community. In Baghdad and other urban cities, brilliant work was carried out in intellectual centers. Working with Jewish and Christian scholars, Muslim thinkers set out to translate and study the works of other great cultures, including Greece and India. Many works of mathematics, medicine, theology and philosophy were translated into the Arabic language. Using these works, the Muslims created their own bodies of original ideas, which they laid out in the many books written during this period.

Among the accomplishments of this period was the development of the Islamic legal system. The basis of this new code was, of course, the Koran and the teachings of Muhammad. Using these two sources as their guide, the scholars worked out a set of laws and regulations that came to be known as the Shari'ah. As they saw it, this was to be the foundation of Islamic society. To enforce these laws and regulations the scholars also worked with the government to establish an Islamic court system. At the head of this new system were the chief judges, the *qadis*.

The Collapse of the Empire

By the middle of the 10th century, the Islamic Empire had given birth to a new and great civilization. The Arabic language and the religion of Islam had taken root throughout the Middle East, North Africa, Spain and Central Asia. Vast numbers of people had converted to Islam and contributed their energy to the new civilization. In law, religion, education, art, science and commerce, the Islamic community was living through a golden age. It was one of the brilliant periods of human history.

Although the cultural achievements during the Abbasid rule would live on, the 10th century brought new political problems that the caliphs proved unable to solve. Preserving the unity of the empire was especially difficult. For more than a century, through diplomacy and the strength of the army, the Abbasid caliphs had controlled the empire. By the 9th century this control began to slip. In North Africa and in other regions, local leaders began to go their own way. Often they continued to recognize the leadership of the caliph while establishing their own rule over a particular region.

By the middle of the 10th century, the caliphs were forced to recognize the end of their power. In 945 a strong army, led by a Persian family named the Buwayhids, swept into Iraq and captured Baghdad. Although they allowed the caliph to retain his official title, they ran the empire.

Another development further divided the Islamic world in the late 10th century. Earlier in the century, a group of Shi'ah had succeeded in establishing a small state in North Africa. From this center of power, they launched attacks to the west, against Egypt. In 969 these leaders, called the Fatimid dynasty, conquered Egypt and established a new city: Cairo, which became their capital. This dynasty would rule Egypt for 200 years, during which it would be in almost constant conflict with the Sunni regions, which were still under the nominal rule of the Abbasid caliphs.

At the height of their power, the Fatimids ruled over a large area that included Egypt, large parts of Syria, Persia, the Arabian Peninsula and North Africa. It became, as a result, a powerful state. Under the Fatimids, Egypt experienced a period of great cultural achievement, and Cairo became a large, bustling city. The Fatimids built a series of mosques and palaces throughout Cairo, many of which can still be seen today.

Among their accomplishments was the creation of the al-Azhar mosque complex—a religious and educational center that would survive the fall of the Fatimid dynasty in the 12th century. Today it is a major university, attracting students from all over the Islamic world. Originally a center of Shi'i education, it is now a center of Sunni thought.

Fatimid rule came to an end in 1171, when Cairo was overrun by the army of Salah al-Din al-Ayyubi, known in the West as Saladin. His victory brought an end to Shi'i rule in Egypt and was warmly welcomed by the inhabitants of Egypt. Most of them had never accepted Shi'i beliefs, preferring to remain Sunnis or Christians. While happy to receive their praises, Salah al-Din had to turn his energies to Jerusalem, then under the rule of the Christian Crusade forces.

The Crusades were a series of campaigns launched over four centuries, beginning with an attack on Jerusalem at the end of the 11th century. Initially the Christian armies succeeded in achieving their goal—the conquest of Jerusalem. This victory, in 1099, was followed by the establishment of small kingdoms along the Mediterranean coast.

The fall of Jerusalem came as a shock to many Muslims. To them, Jerusalem was of great symbolic importance. It was, according to Islamic belief, from Jerusalem that Muhammad had traveled on his miraculous journey to heaven. The Umayyad caliphs had built a famous mosque, the Dome of the Rock, on the site believed to be the place from which Muhammad lifted off on this journey. Many Muslims grew determined to see the city back in Muslim hands.

It fell to Salah al-Din to organize an army to carry out the task. After taking Egypt, he had gone on to conquer Syria and Mesopotamia, thus establishing a unified state. From this position of strength, he sent his army against the Crusaders in 1187. After defeating the Christian army, his troops reestablished Islamic rule over Jerusalem.

Meanwhile, in Baghdad, the Abbasid caliphs continued as mere figureheads. The empire over which the dynasty had once ruled was now broken into many small parts. Most of these states were controlled by military men, who had little interest in religious matters. Deep political and religious differences divided the Islamic community.

During the early part of the 13th century, Mongol armies had been sweeping across the vast lands of China and Russia, moving west into Central Asia. By the 1250s, the Mongols, under their leader Hulagu, moved swiftly through Persia and to the gates of Baghdad. There they demanded complete surrender from the last Abbasid caliph, al-Musta'sim. With few political and no military forces at his disposal, the caliph had little choice but to agree. Baghdad was overrun by the Mongol troops. The caliph and his family were later taken to a small village and executed, bringing a sad end to the once powerful Abbasid caliphate.

Three New Muslim Empires

Never again would one dynasty rule over the whole of the Islamic world. The death of the last Abbasid caliph closed a long and often glorious chapter in the history of Islam. In the heyday of the caliphate, the power, and cultural achievements of the Islamic world were renowned. The political unity of the empire that had made much of this possible was now at an end. What had not ended, however, were the deep spiritual and cultural links between the many regions of the Islamic world.

Even with the achievements of the Abbasid caliphate, the Islamic world had yet to reach its political and cultural peak. The Mongol invasions had been devastating. However, by the 15th century, not only had the Islamic world recovered from the invasions, it had also begun to take great strides forward. With the rise of three new empires, the majority of the regions of Islam now had dynamic political leadership.

At the height of their power, these three states ruled over a vast area stretching from what is known today as Bangladesh west to modern-day Algeria. In the east, ruling over the Indian subcontinent was the Mughal Empire with its capital in Delhi. In Iran, the Safavid dynasty arose to establish a new Shi'i state ruling out of Isfahan. And beginning in the middle of the 14th century, a powerful Turkish state arose in Anatolia known as the Ottoman Empire. At the height of their power, the Ottomans would control an area that included most of North Africa and the Middle East, all of Anatolia, and a large section of southeastern Europe. In 1453, one Ottoman ruler, Mehmet II, laid siege to Constantinople, the capital of the once-great Byzantine Empire. The city fell, and the new Muslim rulers renamed it Istanbul.

The rulers of these three empires were not spiritual guides or teachers in the way Muhammad had been. Their role, at least in theoretical terms, was to uphold the Islamic faith and to see that the lands of Islam were well defended against both internal and external threats. In this way, like the caliphs of old, the Mughal, Safavid and Ottoman rulers had both political and religious responsibilities.

The political power of these dynasties coincided with cultural and economic activity throughout the Islamic world. One of

■ *An elaborately decorated page from a 16th-century Persian book. In many periods of Islamic history, it was common for ruling dynasties to provide patronage to artists, architects, musicians and scholars. One such dynasty, the Safavid, ruled in Iran in the 16th century. The Safavid rulers were known for their love of art and fine architecture.*

the most well-known examples of Islamic architecture, the Taj Mahal, was built by a member of the Mughal dynasty. Like the Mughal rulers, the Safavids also took a keen interest in religious and cultural matters. Abbas I, the greatest of the Safavid leaders, ruled from 1588 to 1629 and did much to promote Iranian art and architecture. Along with magnificent buildings erected in Isfahan, the capital, Iranian artists produced works of calligraphy and miniature painting as well as manuscript illustration. Others in the dynasty also encouraged the work of the religious and legal scholars, many of whom worked as government functionaries in schools, mosques and cultural centers.

The achievements of the Ottoman sultans were no less brilliant. At their peak of prestige, they provided an atmosphere in which scholars, artists, musicians, architects and poets all flourished. The beautiful mosques and other buildings of modern-day Istanbul attest to the cultural environment fostered by these rulers.

This period witnessed a great deal of commercial activity as well. All three dynasties were able to provide the areas under their control with political and economic stability. Throughout this period, merchants bought and sold a great variety of goods—from expensive spices, clothes and jewels, to basic foodstuffs such as rice and wheat. This commerce was carried out within each of the empires as well as across frontiers as great trade caravans and ocean fleets crisscrossed the regions of the Middle East and southern Asia.

This was also a period when the religious scholars, or *ulama* (meaning learned ones), became deeply involved in a wide range of activities—much of this with the blessings of the political rulers. The religious scholars served the community as teachers, prayer leaders and spiritual guides. Some ulama served as local political leaders, voicing the wishes and grievances of their followers to the state. The governments in Isfahan, Istanbul and Delhi all recognized the value of having control over these religious figures. As a result, they employed growing numbers of these men in the government bureaucracy.

Eventually, the ulama became a divided group. Whereas the top scholars—those men with good positions in the bureaucracy—supported the state, other ulama kept their distance from the government. In Iran, especially, the lower ranked members of this religious community refused to serve the state. Some of these men became critics of the political establishment, while many others stayed completely out of politics. Those few who spoke out won the support of the general public.

As with all empires, the days of prestige and power came to an end as strife slowly sapped the strength of all three dynasties.

What were once dynamic states slowly became hollow shells that finally collapsed under the pressures of both internal upheavals and external threats. The Safavid and Mughul states disappeared by the 19th century, while the Ottomans held on until the early part of the 20th century before finally vanishing.

The period from the 15th to the 18th century was a dynamic one for the civilization of Islam. The Mughal, Ottoman, and Safavid empires made a number of remarkable political and cultural achievements. In the frequent periods of stability provided by these states, many parts of the Islamic world reached new levels of prosperity and confidence. Moreover, during this time Islam spread to new regions and more people converted to the faith.

The spread of Islam took place in a variety of ways. Conquests brought new areas under Islamic rule. For example, areas of Central Asia, India and Central Africa were conquered at different times by Muslim forces. Often, these Muslim warriors were fiercely devout and worked hard to encourage local populations to convert. Education and preaching by Muslim missionaries, teachers, holymen and scholars spread Islam to newly conquered areas and to remote parts of previously established Islamic territories. Often these were charismatic men who won people over to Islam through the force of their character and message. Just as often, such missionaries and teachers worked within populations that had long been under Islamic rule but had not yet converted. In Anatolia, for example, under the Ottomans, many Christians converted to Islam.

Just as important was the role played by merchants, who were active during this period. In coastal areas from East Africa to the islands of Indonesia, merchants established contacts with local populations. These social exchanges lead to the establishment of small communities, where missionaries, among others, would come to settle. In this way Islam gradually spread, for example, to the interior regions of Indonesia and Africa.

By the 18th century, Islam had established itself throughout vast areas of Africa and Asia. In many of these regions, Muslims were the dominant majority. Of course differences remained great in languages, local customs and values, eating habits and dress, art and music, and economic systems from one region to the next. Despite these differences, however, strong and lasting bonds developed to tie the disparate Islamic regions together. As Muslims, all the peoples of these regions worshipped the one god, Allah, and venerated his messenger, Muhammad. All prayed toward the sacred city of Mecca and all carried out the other specific rituals expected of Muslims. And, of course, all sought guidance from Islam's great book—the Koran.

■ Interior of a mosque, showing the **mihrab,** or prayer niche, and the **minbar**, or pulpit.

CHAPTER **4**

Koran, Hadith and the Law

Muslims believe that the text of the Koran is the literal Word of God—revealed to Muhammad during his lifetime, written down by his followers under his supervision and put into book form soon after his death. For this reason, the Koran provides the foundation and guiding spirit of Islam.

The Word of God

Muslims become acquainted with the Koran at a young age and many continue to study it throughout their lives. Verses of the book are recited into the ears of babies, and as soon as Muslim children are old enough to speak they begin memorizing and reciting Koranic verses. Muslim children learn to read and write by reciting the book and by copying out verses by hand. As young Muslims approach adulthood, they learn to use the book in prayer. The attachment to the Koran continues until the last days of a Muslim's life, when sections of the book are often read to the dying. Finally, following Islamic tradition, selected passages of the Koran are recited over the grave of a deceased Muslim.

Memorization and recital of the Koran are highly valued activities in the Islamic world. Most Muslim children learn portions of the Koran by heart and use them continually in prayer and on other occasions. Some Muslims go on to memorize the entire book—an act that earns them the respect of their communities. Muslims also place great value in the recitation of the Koran. Throughout the Islamic world, Muslims gather to hear the book recited and show great appreciation for those with particularly well-trained voices.

These recitations are always conducted in Arabic, as it is believed that God revealed the Koran to Muhammad in Arabic: "We have revealed it, a Koran in Arabic, so that you might understand" (XII: 2). For this reason, even the many Muslims who do not speak or read Arabic view that language with great respect.

It is difficult to convey the depth of appreciation and attachment that Muslims feel toward the Koran. For Muslims, the book is a unique event in the history of humankind. It is often described as the one true miracle brought by Muhammad. It is thought that since the Koran represents the Word of God, it is a perfect work. Like God, it is eternal and unchangeable.

The Koran is made up of 114 chapters, known as *surahs*, each of which is made up of a varying number of verses, called *ayahs*. The longest chapter contains 286 verses, the shortest only three. The longer chapters are known as the Medinan chapters because it is believed they were revealed to Muhammad after his arrival in Medina, following his journey from Mecca. The shorter chapters are believed to have been revealed earlier, in Mecca, and are called the Meccan surahs.

The Message of the Koran

According to Islamic tradition, and the Koran itself, the Koran is the last in a series of revelations sent to the world by God. Among His messengers were Moses and the other Hebrew prophets, who brought the Torah, and Jesus Christ, whose followers documented his life and his teachings in the New Testament of the Bible. Like them, Muhammad was the bearer of a divine message—the Koran.

So Muslims do not reject the earlier messages brought by Moses, Jesus and the other prophets that came before Muhammad. On the contrary, the Islamic tradition views these earlier prophets and their messages with great esteem. However, the Koran teaches that over time both the Jewish and Christian scriptures have been corrupted by the men and women who have tried to interpret them.

For example, the Jews and the Christians are criticized in the Koran for having claimed to be a divinely chosen people. The Koran states that only God will decide who, if anyone, is to be chosen and for what reasons. The Christians are also criticized for having thought of Christ as divine. In the view of Muslims, this is to say that God shares his divine nature, or that God has a divine partner. This idea contradicts one of the most fundamental Islamic principles—the absolute oneness of God.

The Koran condemns any individual or group that tries to associate any object or being with God. Muslims use the term *shirk* (associating anything with God) for such an act, which they believe is the one unforgivable sin that humans can commit. Muslims believe that Christians commit an act of shirk when they claim that Jesus is divine.

So, Muslims believe that the role of the Koran is to correct the errors and false ideas that men and women have added to God's

Mā'ida, or The Table Spread.

In the name of Allah, Most Gracious, Most Merciful.

1. O ye who believe !
Fulfil (all) obligations.

2 Lawful unto you (for food)
Are all four-footed animals,
With the exceptions named :
But animals of the chase
Are forbidden while ye
Are in the Sacred precincts
Or in pilgrim garb :
For Allah doth command
According to His Will and Plan.

■ A passage from the fifth chapter, or **surah**, of the Koran. The Koran teaches that it was sent down to Muhammad from God in the Arabic language. Today, the majority of Muslims are not native speakers of Arabic, and therefore the Koran is made available to them in translation.

earlier revelations. As the final revelation from God, it is the most perfect. It was sent to warn humanity that the earlier revelations had been corrupted and to bring people back to the true religion.

God, Humankind, Heaven and Hell

In addition to uniqueness, other characteristics of God are described by the Koran. The first chapter of the book, called *Surat al-Fatihah*, describes some of these qualities:

> *In the name of God, the Merciful, the Compassionate.*
> *All praise belongs to God, the Lord of the Worlds, the*
> *All-Merciful, the All-Compassionate, the Master of the*
> *Day of Judgement. It is You we serve and to You we pray*
> *for support. Guide us on the right path, the path of those*
> *that You have blessed, not that of those with whom You*
> *are angry, nor of those who go astray.* (1.1-7)

According to Islamic tradition, God is, first of all, merciful, ready to forgive the sinner as long as that person repents and turns back to the worship of God and a truly religious life. God is also generous. The Koran speaks often about the bounty of the natural world, given to humanity by God. It says: "God is He Who created the heavens and the earth and sent down water from the clouds, then brought forth with it fruits to sustain you" (14:32).

The greatest proof of God's mercy and compassion, however, are the prophets and the revelation, particularly the prophet Muhammad and the Koran. These provide men and women with the guidance they require to make their way through the world and ultimately to salvation. The revelation, and the teachings of Muhammad, accomplish several tasks: They warn mankind of the evils of sin, they provide knowledge of God and of the proper ways to worship, and they describe the rewards that await the person who follows the revelation and Muhammad's example.

But God is also the Master of the Day of Judgment, whose power and justice are as great as his mercy. For those sinners who repent, God will show forgiveness, but for those sinners who persist in their corrupt ways, God will be unforgiving. There is one verse in the Koran that says that the sinner who attempts to win forgiveness with all the wealth of the world, and even twice that, will fail. God will review their lives on the Day of Judgement and find them unrepentant. Their reward will be the fires of hell.

The Koran offers vivid descriptions of both heaven and hell. In hell the sinner suffers from both physical and mental anguish. While despair and fear fill their hearts and minds, their bodies are tortured with fire and molten metals. A very different experience is promised for those who are saved. Heaven is described in the Koran as a place of rich gardens, with running springs, where the saved will delight in the best of food and drink and the companionship of beautiful young men and women.

In both heaven and hell, humans will be joined by spirits created by God. The spiritual creatures of heaven are the angels. Created out of light, their role is to serve as messengers between God and humanity, delivering the divine revelation to those chosen by God. We have seen that it was the angel Gabriel who brought the revelation from God to Muhammad in the cave at Hira. Below the angels are the jinn, who are made of fire and who can be either good or bad. Like human beings, these fiery spirits will be judged by God at the end of time and sent either to heaven or hell. In the period before Islam, the jinn were thought to inhabit rocks and trees. With the establishment of Islam, this belief was incorporated into the new religion, and it was said that these spirits lived in heaven.

In hell, the sinners are joined by Satan and his followers. The story of Satan, who is known as Iblis in the Islamic tradition, is one of the most vivid parts of the Koran. It begins with an affirmation of the special relationship that exists between humankind and God. God created people to serve as his representatives on earth. At the moment of creation, God summons the angels to inform them of humanity's special quality. He orders them to bow down before the first of humans, Adam. As the following passage from the Koran describes, Iblis angrily refuses, and God casts him out of heaven for disobeying the divine command:

> Then all the angels bowed together, except Iblis, who refused
> to join those who were bowing. God said: Oh, Iblis, why are
> you not among those who are upon their knees?' He said:
> 'I am not going to kneel before a being formed out of clay,

of shaped mud.' God said: Then leave here, you are cast out,
and indeed you are cursed until the Day of Judgement.'
He said: 'My Lord, spare me until the Day of Resurrection.'
God said: 'You may join those waiting for that appointed day.'
He said: Since you have made evil of me, I will certainly make
the world attractive to those on earth, and I will make evil of
all of them, except those of them who are your sincere followers.'
God said: 'This is the path that leads directly to me. As for my
followers, you will have no influence over them except those
who go astray to follow you, and surely Hell will be the place
for them.'   (15.30-43)

The Koran clearly states that God expects humans to perform the rituals of Islam and read the Koran. But it also provides guidelines for living life as a Muslim. According to the Koran, human beings are each responsible for their own actions and thoughts. Consequently, the decision to follow the true path of God, to live a sincerely religious life, is up to each individual. Those who choose to do so will win God's mercy, and those who do not will earn only his anger.

The Muslim Community and the Koran

The devout Muslim is not only an individual but also a member of the Islamic community. That community has the responsibility to follow God's will, which means to uphold the teachings of the Koran. As the Koran says, God made the Muslims into a particular community, or ummah, just as he had earlier done with the Jews and Christians. He expects that community to act as an example to all other communities.

To guide the community the Koran provides regulations that every Muslim is expected to follow. These include not only the ritual duties of prayer but also rules regarding inheritance, marriage and other aspects of life. Over the course of Islamic history, these rules have become the basis of Islamic law. The Koran says that the goal of the Muslim community is to create a just society. So the Koran not only teaches human beings about God, Muhammad and the revelation, it also serves as a specific guide to the community of Muslims on how to follow God from day to day.

■ *A page from a 13th-century Koran. Muslims believe that the Koran is the last and most perfect of God's revelations to humankind. The Koran is made up of 114 **surahs**, or chapters, each of which consists of one or more verses, known as **ayahs**.*

The Koran is not an easy book to understand. In fact, there are many passages that require much study before their meaning becomes clear. Since Muslims throughout the ages have sought guidance from the Koran, it has always been important for them to know what the book is teaching. As a result, those who study the Koran are looked to by other Muslims for guidance. Often these people became teachers in their local communities.

Studying and explaining the Koran became, very early on, an important branch of Islamic education and intellectual life. *Tafsir* is the term used by Muslims for Koranic interpretation or explanation. In the 9th and 10th centuries, Muslim scholars spent years studying the verses of the Koran. The best of these scholars produced multivolume works—still used today in universities throughout the Islamic world—in which they laid out their detailed interpretations. Perhaps the most famous of these works was written in the early 10th century by a scholar in Baghdad named Abu Ja'far Muhammad ibn Jarir al-Tabari (d. 923).

Although the Koran embodies the teachings of Islam, there is another source of guidance they look to as well—the life and teachings of Muhammad. No individual is viewed with the same awe and respect by Muslims as Muhammad ibn Abd Allah. In countless biographies and poems, Muslims have spoken of their profound attachment to the Prophet. He is revered by Muslims for his special relationship to God. Like the prophets before him, he was selected to bring the divine message to mankind. However, Muhammad is thought to have been closer to God than were any of the other prophets. He was the one chosen to bring the Koran to humanity. For that reason, his relationship to God was unique.

Muhammad and Hadith

Muhammad is also revered by Muslims for having lived a remarkable life. Muslim descriptions of Muhammad portray him as a man of compassion, great intelligence and honesty. A gifted political leader, Muhammad turned a small group of followers into a powerful community, the foundation of an expanding empire. A skilled military chief, he led his followers to victory against more powerful enemies, eventually gaining control of the entire Arabian Peninsula.

Above all, Muhammad was a teacher of great wisdom. There are many accounts in the biographies of Muhammad that tell of people who converted to Islam after hearing him speak. These were people who did not understand the words of the Koran or who doubted the truth of the book. With great patience and care, Muhammad was able to bring them into the community of believers.

For all these reasons, it was not long before Muhammad was seen by his followers as a model human being. For them and for the generations of Muslims after them, he became the example for all Muslims to follow—not only an exemplary human being, but even incapable of error of any kind.

Even during Muhammad's lifetime, Muslims began to collect stories of his activities and teachings. His closest followers—

those who had observed Muhammad on a daily basis for years—passed on these stories to others after his death. These accounts, known as Hadith, grew very popular and soon were circulating throughout the Islamic community.

As the Hadith began to circulate through the community, Muslims listened with great interest. These reports were passed on from person to person, community to community, in both written and oral form through the centuries. From the Hadith, Muslims learned about Muhammad's accomplishments as a military and political leader as well as details of his private life. For instance, there are accounts of Muhammad's methods of battle and diplomacy as well as descriptions of his religious activities and family life. No Muslim could ever hope to be like Muhammad in every way, but many Muslims believe that if one strives to follow Muhammad's example, one will live a pious and meaningful life.

Within 200 years of Muhammad's death, the numbers of Hadith circulating around the Islamic community probably were in the hundreds of thousands. By that time, the Islamic empire had spread well beyond the limits of the Arabian Peninsula. In the areas conquered by the Muslim armies large numbers of people had converted to Islam. Like those before them, these new Muslims were eager to learn about Muhammad and his teachings. This increased even further the demand for the Hadith.

By this period it became obvious to many in the Islamic community that most of these reports about Muhammad were fabrications; that they had been created after Muhammad's death by members of the community who claimed that they had heard the reports from someone who had recorded them in the time of the prophet. Very often those who made up these reports were well-meaning Muslims who thought that their act of fabrication was a sign of their reverence for Muhammad. Others had created new Hadith in an attempt to put forth their own answers to problems facing the early Muslim community. While no one was punished for this activity, it became clear that the fabricated reports would have to be weeded out. After all, if the community was going to use the Hadith as a source of guidance, it would have to be sure that only the true Hadith were being used.

In order to find the true Hadith, Muslim scholars began to examine large numbers of these reports. Since the empire had grown so large, scholars often had to travel vast distances in order to collect the many accounts. Gradually, the scholars were able to distinguish the real Hadith from the fabricated ones. Out of this exhausting effort came a number of collections of Hadith that were considered reliable.

As time went on, six of these collections were shown preference by the scholarly community of Islam and became the standard works of Hadith—still read today by students and scholars in universities throughout the Islamic world.

The early Muslim community read and memorized the Koran and Hadith, much as Muslims continue to do today. The scholars of the early community also put the Koran and Hadith to work to develop Islamic law, or the Shari'ah. Although the term is often translated as holy law, a better way to interpret it is probably "the way ordained by God."

The Law of God

For Muslims, the Shari'ah is the divine plan for the Islamic community. It lays out the regulations and duties that all Muslims are expected to follow during the course of their lives, including the rituals that Muslims are expected to perform when worshipping God as well as the regulations for behavior with one's family and in society.

The Shari'ah developed from the deeply felt needs of the early Muslims. The conquests had transformed the small community in Medina into a powerful empire. For many Muslims, however, the riches of the empire were only of secondary importance. The first priority was the assurance of a moral Islamic community. If it was to follow the Word of God and the teachings of Muhammad, these Muslims said, it needed a body of Islamic law.

From the 8th to the start of the 10th century, scholars of Islam worked at the difficult process of developing this body of law. One problem they faced was the difficulty of many passages in the Koran that were interpreted in different ways by different scholars, resulting in arguments and disputes. The Koran, moreover, did not contain answers—even partial answers—to all the questions they faced. In those cases where even the Hadith did not provide answers, the scholars were obliged to come to a solution by using their own opinions guided as closely as possible by the principles of the Koran and Hadith.

By the beginning of the 10th century, the legal experts had reached their goal: The basic elements of the Shari'ah were in place. This code of regulations set out in legal manuals written by the various scholars and their students, showed that the disagreements between the different groups of legal scholars had not disappeared. On certain issues of law, such as how divorce between a husband and wife could be achieved and how the property of a deceased person was to be divided between the person's heirs, the scholars had reached conflicting conclusions about what the Koran and Hadith permitted. These differences led to the emergence of various schools of Islamic law.

The Schools of Law

The schools all developed in the same way: A gifted scholar would set out his ideas in his classes and writings; his students would refine these and pass them on to their students, who would in turn do the same. In the early period, a number of these schools came into being, but most of them dissolved quickly. The few that survived were named after the men around whom the schools had first formed.

The two oldest Sunni legal schools are called Hanafi and Maliki. The former was named after Abu Hanifa (d. 767), a legal scholar who lived and worked in the Iraqi city of Kufah. He acquired a reputation among scholars for his liberal views on the law and for his great intelligence. Some of the greatest legal scholars of the following generation were his students. The Hanafi school is currently dominant in India, Central Asia, Turkey and parts of Egypt.

The Maliki school took its name from Malik ibn Anas (d. 796), a scholar from the city of Medina—the first capital of the Islamic empire and the center of vigorous work by legal and religious scholars. Malik was one of the most highly respected of these men. He is known to the present day for his dedication to collecting Hadith and for writing the *al-Muwatta*—one of the most

■ *The interior of a mosque in the Pakistani city of Sukkur, located along the Indus River. Mosques throughout the Islamic world are used for prayer, study and contemplation. During the month-long fast of Ramadan, it is common for Muslims, usually men, to spend long hours in the mosque, reading, praying and quietly conversing.*

influential early books on the law. The Maliki school is currently dominant in North and central Africa.

Perhaps the greatest legal scholar in Islamic history was Muhammad ibn Idris al-Shafi'i, who gave his name to the Shafi'i school of law, which is currently followed in Malaysia, southern Arabia and East Africa. He was born in Palestine and studied in various parts of the Middle East, including Medina, where he studied under the great Malik ibn Anas. He then taught in Baghdad and later Egypt, where he died in 819. Al-Shafi'i laid out his ideas on the law in the *Risalah*—one of the most renowned books of the early period of Islam.

In his book, al-Shafi'i argued persuasively that after the Koran the most important source for legal scholars to use in reaching their decisions was the Hadith. It was to a great extent because of this argument that the Hadith became so highly regarded by all Muslims. With al-Shafi'i's work, the stature of Muhammad rose to new heights. Like Abu Hanifa, al-Shafi'i attracted many fine students, some of whom went on to contribute to the development of Islamic law.

The last of the Sunni legal schools to emerge was the Hanbali school—named after Ahmad ibn Hanbal (d. 855), who was a younger contemporary of al-Shafi'i in Baghdad. Early on, Ibn Hanbal acquired the reputation for being outspoken and very conservative. Frequently he had bitter arguments with other scholars over a variety of religious and legal issues. He even became involved in an angry dispute with the court and at one point was arrested and beaten for his opinions. This helped to strengthen his following among students and younger scholars who shared his views. Today the only area where the Hanbali school is dominant is in the modern state of Saudi Arabia.

Besides the schools of legal thought in the Sunni Muslim community, there is the Shi'i law school, which is known as the Ja'firi school. It was named after a great Shi'i scholar who lived and taught in Medina and later in Baghdad: Ja'far al-Sadiq. In his early career, al-Sadiq lived a quiet life, writing and holding classes for his students. In 750, the Abbasids swept into power, and in a short time the quiet of al-Sadiq's life was shattered.

Al-Sadiq was by that time one of the leading members of the Shi'i community. This status was not entirely to his liking. The new Abbasid caliphs, from the very start of their rule, viewed the Shi'ah as political rivals and thus kept a very close eye on al-Sadiq and other Shi'i leaders. Although al-Sadiq had always been careful to stay out of politics—partly for fear that he would end up like Husayn—the second Abbasid caliph, al-Mansur, ordered al-Sadiq arrested on several occasions. Al-Sadiq died in the year 765, and it was believed by many that he was poisoned on the orders of the caliph.

For the Shi'ah, this was only one more example of the oppression they had come to expect from the Sunni community. Al-Sadiq's death would drive one more wedge between the two Muslim communities.

CHAPTER 5

The Variety of Religious Life in Islam

Every one of the world's religious communities has been torn by internal conflict. For different reasons, Christians have turned against Christians, Jews against Jews, and Muslims against Muslims. Sometimes, solutions were found to end such conflicts; too often, however, permanent division into different sects resulted. While continuing to belong to the same large community, the members of each sect also held on to certain beliefs not shared by the other sects.

The Sects of Islam

The division of the Islamic community into the Sunni and Shi'i sects began with the deaths of Ali, in 661, and his son Husayn, in 680. Deprived of their leaders, the Shi'ah grew frustrated as the Umayyads took over the caliphate. Despite the loss of Ali and Husayn, many of the Shi'ah remained loyal to the Alid family.

The title given by the Shi'ah to Ali, his two sons and a select group of men who came after them was Imam. Following Husayn's brutal murder, the Shi'ah agreed that the position of Imam should go to a member of the Alid family. But which one?

A number of the Shi'ah argued that the new Imam was now Husayn's son, Ali, the only of Husayn's male offspring to survive the massacre at Karbala. Ali, known also as Zayn al-Abidin, was then a respected scholar, esteemed for his deep piety. But others of the Shi'ah had another choice in mind. This disagreement led to a division within the Shi'i community. Although a number remained faithful to Ali, the son of Husayn, others threw their loyalty behind a third son of Ali ibn Abi Talib; a man named Muhammad ibn al-Hanafiyyah.

Ibn al-Hanafiyyah was then in the eye of a political storm. In the city of Kufah, a center of Shi'i activity, a revolt against the Umayyads was brewing. Leading the revolt was Mukhtar al-Thaqafi, a follower of the Alid family. He had called on the Shi'ah to join him in overthrowing the Umayyads in the name of Ibn al-Hanafiyyah. The revolt soon went badly for the Shi'ah when Mukhtar and many of the rebels fell in battle in 687. Ibn al-Hanafiyyah, who had never actually joined the revolt, lived until the year 700. In the meantime, Ali Zayn al-Abidin had kept clear of politics, preferring teaching and writing to armed rebellion, until his death in 712.

Once again, the Shi'ah—including the followers of Ibn al-Hanafiyyah and Ali Zayn al Abidin—faced the problem of finding a new Imam. As before, they could not agree on which Alid to choose as their next leader. A number of small Shi'i sects appeared, each with its own candidate for Imam. This pattern of disagreement over the successor of a deceased Imam would repeat itself frequently over the next 200 years. Most of these groups were small and disappeared quickly. Only a handful of them survived this early period.

The Shi'i Sects

Of these various branches of the Shi'ah, the earliest to emerge was the Zaydi sect. Zayd ibn Ali, after whom this sect is named, was the son of Ali Zayn al-Abidin. Unlike his father, Zayd was willing to fight for the rights of the Alid family. In 740, he organized a rebellion in Kufah against the Umayyads. As with Husayn years earlier, the Kufans promised their support to Zayd. Once again, at the crucial moment, the Kufans backed out. The

Umayyad soldiers overwhelmed Zayd's followers, killing Zayd in the process.

Despite his death, the followers of Zayd remained active. Led by other members of the Alid family, one group of Zaydis settled in northern Iran, where they established a small state that survived into the 11th century. Other Zaydis made their way to Yemen in southwestern Arabia. The state they established there would have a long, frequently violent history throughout which the Zaydis maintained their presence. In the early part of the 20th century, the leaders of this Zaydi community were able to create an independent state that lasted into the 1960s, before succumbing to revolution.

The history of another sect of the Shi'ah was no less eventful. The Isma'ili Shi'ah emerged after the death of the man they looked to as their Imam. Isma'il ibn Ja'far was the son of the famous Shi'i scholar, Ja'far al-Sadiq, a great-grandson of the famous Husayn. Although he died at a fairly young age, Isma'il was seen by a number of Shi'ah as their Imam. They transferred their loyalties to his son Muhammad ibn Isma'il and then to his descendants.

The Isma'ilis, like the Zaydis, showed a great deal of resourcefulness in spreading their doctrines. Organized in small cells, Isma'ili activists moved into various regions to form small communities. The movement broke apart in the 9th century when one of its leading activists, Ubayd Allah, claimed that he was the new Imam. Rejected by the other Isma'ilis, he and his followers went to the area of North Africa known today as Tunisia. In a mountainous area, Ubayd Allah and his men organized a small army. They then overthrew the Abbasid governor who controlled the area. The result was the birth of the Fatimid dynasty.

Some 200 years later, in the 11th century, another break occurred within the Isma'ili sect. A new movement emerged that came to be known as the Druze. Today the Druze number roughly 300,000 and live in Syria, Israel and Lebanon. Many Muslims believe that the Druze hold ideas that violate the basic tenets of Islam and for this reason should not be considered part of the Islamic community.

Another small Shi'i sect that emerged during the medieval period is the Nusayri sect, known also as the Alawi. This sect,

■ **Imam**

*In the Sunni Muslim community, the term **imam** is used in different ways. It is used to address respected religious scholars and teachers. Early in their history, the Sunnis also used it to address the Abbasid caliphs. It is used today for the individual who leads prayer sessions in the mosque. The Shi'ah use it to refer to Ali, his sons and the men who succeeded them to the leadership of the Shi'i community.*

which continues to exist today, has lived for centuries in small villages in northern Syria. The present ruler of Syria, Hafiz al-Asad, is an Alawi as are members of his government and top officers of the military. There is much opposition within Syria today to the Asad regime; one reason for this is the resentment felt by the Sunni majority over being ruled by a minority that does not share its beliefs.

The most important of the Shi'i sects is known in Arabic as the Ithna Ashariyyah; in English, the Twelver Shi'ah. Today, the Twelvers form a majority in Iran and are present in large numbers in Lebanon, Kuwait, and Iraq. With little doubt, the most prominent member of this sect today is the man who led the 1979 Islamic Revolution in Iran, the Ayatollah Khomeini. Before his death in June 1989, he had become one of the most controversial figures in recent world history.

The Twelve Imams

As the name of the sect indicates, the Twelvers believe that the position of Imam passed from Ali ibn Abi Talib down through a chain of eleven other men, all descendants of Ali's family. With Ali these men numbered 12 in all. Among them were Ali ibn Abi Talib and his two sons, Hasan and Husayn, who were the second and third Imams after their father. The fourth Imam was Ali Zayn al-Abidin, and the sixth was the renowned Ja'far al-Sadiq. Famous for his deep piety and brilliant scholarship, he was responsible for developing many of the doctrines of the Twelver sect. These doctrines centered on the figure of the Imam. According to the Twelvers, the Imams possessed certain distinguishing characteristics.

First, the Imams were divinely inspired. Like Muhammad, they are believed to have had a close relationship with God. In the books of Twelver scholars, the Imams are referred to as The Proof of God or The Sign of God. These titles are used to show that the Imams are God's representatives on earth and that devotion to the Imams is required of all.

Unlike Muhammad, the Imams did not carry a divine message to humankind. But in so far as the Imams were the providers of spiritual guidance, they were considered the direct heirs to

Muhammad's legacy. Some Twelver writers have described the Imams as having been created out of the same substance as Muhammad. The substance is described as a brilliant light created by God before the creation of the world. From this divine light, God is believed to have created Muhammad and the Imams as well as Fatima.

The Twelvers also believed that each of the Imams was appointed by the Imam before him. Just as Ali had appointed Hasan, Hasan appointed Husayn, and so on. This idea grew from the belief that Muhammad had chosen Ali as his successor in a sermon he gave at the end of his life. In his sermon, Muhammad reportedly told the Muslims gathered before him that upon his death they were to follow Ali. Although Sunni Muslims deny this ever took place, the Shi'ah believe that it did, and for them it is an event of great significance.

The Imams, according to the Twelvers, possessed two other characteristics as well. First, they were incapable of error or sin. Second, the Imams were in possession of a special body of knowledge, which they received from God through Muhammad, that allowed them to serve as the spiritual and political leaders of the community.

These were characteristics possessed by all twelve of the Imams. Clearly, in the eyes of the Shi'ah they were unique and remarkable human beings. Of the twelve there was one who stood out among all the others: the Twelfth Imam.

■ *Fatima*
As the daughter of the Prophet, the wife of Ali ibn Abi Talib and the mother of Hasan and Husayn, Fatima is highly revered by not only the Twelvers but by other Shi'ah as well. The Fatimid Shi'ah, in fact, named themselves after her.

The Twelfth Imam

In 874, Hasan al-Askari, the Eleventh Imam, suddenly died in the city of Samarra—then the capital of the Abbasid Caliphate. Just as had happened after the deaths of the other Imams, the Shi'i community argued over who was the successor to al-Askari. Some said it was his brother Ja'far; others disagreed. The Twelvers had their own opinion.

They insisted that al-Askari had an infant son whom he had chosen to succeed him. This was the first that many in the Shi'i community had heard of the boy, so they reacted with skepticism. How were they to know he existed? The response came that to reveal his identity was to risk having the boy and the whole Shi'i community attacked by the Abbasid authorities. While the Shi'ah were less politically active than they had been in earlier periods, they were still viewed with suspicion by the Abbasids. For this reason, it was considered unwise to reveal the identity of the new Imam.

While many expressed doubts about this mysterious child, the majority of Shi'ah slowly came to accept the idea that he had become the new Imam, and the notion that he was in hiding until some future time. Thus he was given the title of the Hidden Imam. The scholars of the Twelver community taught that he had gone into hiding in a small cave in Samarra. Today, Shi'ah still gather in the small mosque located over this cave to pray for his return.

Following the disappearance of the Twelfth Imam, many in the Twelver community began to wonder when he would come out of hiding. When asked, the Twelver scholars said that the Twelfth Imam would emerge from hiding when he was summoned by God; in other words, at the end of time.

■ *A member of a nomadic tribe of southern Tunisia. She is wearing jewelry commonly found in many parts of North Africa and the Middle East. On her necklace hangs the "Hand of Fatima," a symbol of good fortune. In many parts of the Islamic world, as in large areas of the non-Islamic world, the freedom of women, especially those of poorer classes, are sharply limited.*

On that Last Day, the scholars explained, the Hidden Imam will reappear in a burst of celestial light. He will stand at the head of an army of angels and of all the Shi'ah who over the centuries followed the Imams faithfully. He will be wearing Muhammad's sandals and ring, and in his hand he will wield Muhammad's sword. His destination will be Mecca, then Medina, then the remainder of the world. In each of these places he will promise eternal life to those who were faithful to the Imams. And, with great violence, he will then turn against those who had oppressed the Imams and the community of Shi'ah.

The term used for the Hidden Imam is *al-Mahdi*, or "the one guided by God." In his role as the Mahdi, the Twelfth Imam is expected to bring a new social order to the world—an eternal age of justice in which the sufferings of the Shi'i community will end. As we have seen, the Shi'ah were a minority in the Islamic community and, too often, a persecuted minority. They had seen their leaders killed and imprisoned; moreover, early in their history, they had attempted several revolts against the rule of the Umayyad and Abbasid caliphs, only to see these revolts harshly put down. It is believed that with his armies of angels and followers, rising up with him on that chosen day, the Hidden Imam will finally end the suffering of the Shi'i community. He will then rule with justice and wisdom over that community until the Day of Judgment, when God will decide on the fate of each and every being.

Disagreement between the Sunnis and the Shi'ah

Held dear by the Twelver Shi'ah, these ideas about the Imams were never accepted by the Sunni community. In fact, such notions were a major cause of the division between the two communities.

For the Shi'ah, political and religious leadership could only come from one source: the Imams. The Twelfth Imam would eventually return to right all the wrongs of the world. For these reasons, the Imams—and they alone—could serve as the proper leaders of the community.

The Sunnis had a different idea of leadership. They respected the Imams as men of great learning, but they could not accept that the Imams were inspired by God. Nor could they agree that the Imams were the direct heirs of Muhammad. For the Sunnis, the leaders of the community were the caliphs.

It was not believed that the caliphs were divinely inspired or in possession of special knowledge of any kind. They were simply human beings chosen to lead the community in this world: to defend the community from internal and external enemies and to uphold the Shari'ah. They were never considered a source of religious guidance in the way the Imams were by the Shi'ah.

Another major disagreement between the Shi'ah and the Sunnis was over the idea of salvation. The Islamic community, it was believed, would only win God's mercy on the Day of Judgment if the community as a whole lived according to God's law. For the Sunnis, the Shari'ah, as the embodiment of God's law, had to be respected and followed by all. The caliphs were there only to defend the Shari'ah and to protect the community, not to lead the community to salvation. Only the entire Islamic community working as a whole could achieve this goal.

For the Shi'ah, the quest for salvation lay not with the community but with the Imams. Without them it could never hope to win God's mercy; only the Imams could lead the Islamic community along the right path.

During the years that each of the Imams lived and taught within the community, the Shi'ah could turn to them for guidance. This changed, however, when the Twelfth Imam disappeared. The Shi'ah now faced a troubling question. If the Imams were the only true guides of the community, then what was to happen when the last of the Imams was no longer present? If no Imam was present, then what was to prevent the Shi'ah from losing faith in the Imams and in their religious beliefs? And who was to speak for the community in times of trouble?

Answers to these questions came from the scholars of the Twelver community: the ulama. They argued that they would carry out the functions of the Hidden Imam until such time as God decides that the Hidden Imam should return. This did not mean the scholars were claiming themselves as equal to the Imams. Rather, as they put it, they would represent the Imam until his return, when they will hand over these responsibilities to him.

The Scholars of the Twelver Shi'ah

These ideas were developed over a long period, from roughly the end of the 11th century into the 19th century and up to the present day. The Twelver ulama, especially the leading members, became very influential. These men at the top of a hierarchy of scholars wielded a great deal of power—especially in Iran, where a large proportion of the populace eventually converted to the Twelver Shi'i sect.

For a time, the political power of the Twelver scholars was limited, mainly because Iran was under the rule of Sunni leaders who wanted to keep power out of the hands of the Shi'ah. This changed in the 16th century with the rise of the Shi'i Safavid dynasty, which gave the ulama the opportunity to influence

■ The shrine of the Kadimayn in Baghdad, Iraq. The shrine is the site of the tombs of the 7th and 9th Imams of the Twelver Shi'i Muslim sect. Built in the 10th century, it has been enlarged and redecorated at different times in its history. Shi'i Muslims perform pilgrimage to this and other important shrines like it.

political decisions. However, they disagreed among themselves over how involved in politics they should become. Moreover, despite their acceptance of Twelver doctrines, the leaders of the new dynasty were concerned that the ulama would gain too much power; they determined not to let that happen.

In the meantime, the ulama continued to debate the question of their involvement in politics. Some said that politics should be avoided and that the ulama should concentrate on religious activities. Others argued that by increasing their political involvement the ulama could work toward limiting the corrupt activities of the state. Still others maintained that political activity was fine but not if it meant serving the government. The role of the ulama, in their view, should be to support the state when it ruled justly but to attack it when it became tyrannical. Above all, they said, the religious leadership should maintain its independence from the government.

While this debate among the ulama continued, Iran's political landscape changed. The Safavids were overthrown in the middle of the 18th century. The new rulers, the Qajars, were also Shi'ah; like the Safavids, however, they were wary of the ulama becoming too powerful and therefore sought to keep the scholarly community at bay. To do so, they placed a number of ulama in government positions. Although on the surface this move seemed contrary to the rulers' purpose, it actually served them quite well. Through these appointed officials they were able to keep a close eye on the ulama and their activities. The appointments also enabled Iran's rulers to claim they had the support of the scholarly community. The tensions between the state and Iran's religious leaders remained, however.

At the start of the 20th century, the Qajars were replaced by a new power: the Pahlavi dynasty. The founder of the dynasty was a violent-tempered officer named Reza Khan, who set out to create a centralized state in Iran. To control the religious community, Reza Khan instituted policies that strictly limited the activities of the ulama.

For a time, Reza Khan was successful in controlling Iran's religious leaders. His policies, however, angered many Iranians. As Reza Khan, and then his son Muhammad, continued to pursue these policies, hostility to the dynasty grew. By the 1960s, these tensions would reach the point of explosion.

The Ascetics of Islam

The division of the early Islamic community into sects had come out of conflicts over matters of religion and politics. At the same time, the early community was facing another kind of conflict—not of sword and fire but of spiritual beliefs.

The successes of the early Islamic community had been startling. In a relatively short time, the once small and vulnerable community had spread beyond Arabia into the regions of the Middle East, Central Asia and North Africa. With the conquest of these large territories had also come new levels of wealth. This was especially true of the Muslim military and political elite, who gained control of large cities, most of which were important commercial centers. Thus, they were able to expand and benefit from trade. They also accumulated wealth by imposing heavy taxes on the people of these conquered cities. As they prospered, the elites of Islamic society, including the caliphs, lived in great luxury.

However, not all Muslims shared this taste for the good life. As the empire grew, some Muslims began to ask difficult questions: How should Muslims live? What kind of society were Muslims going to build out of their new empire? Was success in this world a proper concern for Muslims? What of the teachings of Muhammad and the Koran? For these Muslims, material possessions and political power meant little if the deeper truths of the Koran and the teachings of Muhammad were ignored. Increasingly they turned away from the riches enjoyed by others around them to lead simple lives. They wore plain clothing and shunned the pursuit of money. Many saw poverty as a necessity. They dedicated themselves to the worship of God through meditation and prayer. In pursuing this way of life, they became the first ascetics of Islam.

The models for these early ascetics were Muhammad and the first leaders of the community, men like Abu Bakr. Muhammad, they believed, had led a simple life of devotion to God. He had not permitted himself to be tempted by the luxuries of this world.

After him, Abu Bakr had also shunned wealth, preferring to live in a state of poverty and deep religious devotion. This was how the ascetics sought to lead their lives.

For these devout early Muslims the greatest concern was God, whom they believed to be not only the creator of the universe but also the object of profound devotion and love. In different ways, the ascetics expressed this deep attachment to God.

One of the earliest voices of asceticism in Islam was that of Hasan al-Basri (d. 728). Theologian and teacher, al-Basri was famous for his powerful sermons. He is said to have warned his listeners that the world was a wretched place in which too many people had forgotten God. Stories circulated after his death of how he would spend long hours weeping, not only because of the state of the world but also out of fear of God's wrath on the day of judgment.

Not all the early ascetics were as gloomy; others thought of God with a profound sense of love. Rabia al-Adawiyyah (d. 801) was one such individual. Like al-Basri, she lived a simple life, shunning fine clothes and property. But her approach to the worship of God was very different. She described God in joyful language. It was as if she were describing the emotions of a human being in love, although for al-Adawiyyah this was a far greater love. It is believed that she received during her lifetime many marriage proposals from men of her community and that she said no to each of them, claiming that her love was reserved for God.

The Rise of Sufism

Al-Basri, al-Adawiyyah and others like them attracted followers who shared their ideas and came to learn from them. These individuals, in turn, attracted students of their own, and in this way, the ideas of asceticism and absolute devotion to God spread through the Islamic community.

These ideas and practices gave birth to Islamic mysticism, which is known as Sufism. The mystics, or Sufis, followed in the footsteps of the early ascetics, but they may also have absorbed the teachings of Christian and Jewish mystics living in areas of the Middle East. For several generations, they developed their ideas

■ Sufism

The term **Sufism** probably comes from the Arabic word for wool, **suf.** It is thought that the early Muslim ascetics wore garments made from rough wool. These plain, unfinished garments were meant to symbolize the rejection of the luxuries and concerns of this world. The Muslim ascetics may have copied this practice from Christian monks living in the Middle East when Islam spread through the region.

into more formal practices. It is important to note that Sufism is not a sect of Islam; it has been and still is practiced by both the Sunnis and Shi'ah.

For the Sufis, nothing was more important than the presence of God in the world.

The Sufis saw life as a kind of journey in which one was constantly seeking a direct experience of God. Many of them believed that the way to seek that experience was to study the Koran and the Hadith and to pray regularly—in short, to live the simple and disciplined life of a devout Muslim. Other Sufis disagreed, however. They felt that although prayer, the study of the Koran and other duties of Muslims were necessary to a religious life, these practices were not enough. They sought a more direct and emotional experience of God.

At first, the number of Sufis was very small. Usually they were scholars who spent their days in private, discussing the nature of the spiritual life and the various ritual practices that could bring one closer to God. Their ideas were beyond the understanding of the average person and thus in the beginning had little popular appeal. Gradually, however, as the Sufis began to attract students and followers, these mystics and holymen and holywomen began to be seen as people with unusual spiritual powers.

As the ideas and ritual practices developed by the Sufis spread, informal study groups gathered in mosques or homes. By the start of the 10th century Sufi centers were established, in which a Sufi master would serve as teacher and leader to followers. Some of these followers would go on to become teachers themselves, and many of their students would do the same in their turn. Thus, Sufism was passed on from generation to generation.

By the 12th century, Sufi centers could be found in cities, towns, and many rural areas throughout the Middle East and North Africa. These centers often included schools, mosques and hostels where students could find a meal and a place to sleep. The heart of these centers was the house of the Sufi master, or *shaykh*. It was there where the shaykh would conduct classes and lead followers through ritual practices.

The Sufi Orders

By the 12th century, the casual gatherings of the earlier period had evolved into formal organizations called Sufi orders. Each Sufi order, or *tariqah*, was built on the teachings of an early master and the students of that person. Their ideas and the rituals they used became formalized into specific forms of worship. Often the Sufi order would bear the name of its founder—usually the original master or an early student.

One of the earliest of the Sufi orders was the Qadiriyah, named after Abd al-Qadir al-Jilani (d. 1166). Of Iranian descent, Abd al-Qadir had been a legal scholar in Baghdad for many years. Only late in life did he begin to teach his Sufi ideas in public. His following quickly grew, and a center was opened for him. Following his death, his closest students continued to teach his ideas and open Qadiriyah centers throughout the Middle East.

Other orders were also established during the 12th and 13th centuries. The Suhrawardiyah order, for example, took its name from Umar ibn Abd Allah al-Suhrawardi (d. 1234), a religious scholar from the small Iranian town of Suhraward. Centers of this order were set up throughout Iran, Central Asia, and India. Another example, the Shadhiliyah order, was founded in North Africa by Ahmad ibn Abd Allah al-Shadhili (d. 1258). Born in Morocco and educated in Egypt, he attracted a large following in Egypt and later in Tunis, where he died. Centers of his order were soon present from Syria and Arabia across North Africa to Morocco.

By the 14th and 15th centuries, these and other Sufi orders were so widespread that they had considerable political power. Frequently, governments in different regions of the Islamic world worked to win the support of the Sufi orders. The Safavid dynasty—which combined Sufism and radical Shi'i ideas and ruled Iran from the late 15th to the early 18th century— began as a Sufi movement.

Sufi orders played an important part in spreading Islam to new regions of the world. In India and areas of Central Asia, Malaysia and Indonesia, plus large parts of sub-Saharan Africa, Sufi missionaries converted numerous people to Islam. Sufis accompanied merchants as they plied their trade across the Indian

A Persian miniature of the 16th century. The scene of a prince's court is depicted with remarkable attention to detail. Musicians entertain the prince and his entourage, while over a small bluff, onlookers stare with great curiosity.

Ocean to various regions of Asia and across the trade routes of the African continent. They even marched with armies of various Islamic dynasties that widened the area of their control through conquest. In each region, Sufi orders would set up centers where they would spread the message of Islam.

CHAPTER 6

Muslim Ritual Life

As with the members of other religious communities, each Muslim is expected to carry out religious rituals that serve the ultimate goal of worshipping God. But more is expected of the Muslim than the mere practice of rituals. The practice must be accompanied by intention, or what Muslims call *niyyah*. Whether it is prayer or pilgrimage, the believer must perform each act of worship with full sincerity. Going through the rituals without concentrating on their true meaning is little more than not carrying them out at all.

The most important of the ritual practices performed by Muslims are often called the Five Pillars of Islam. The first of these is *salat*, or daily prayer. Muslims carry out the salat five times daily. Each session of prayer begins with the call or summons to worship.

Prayer and Shahadah

For many non-Muslims who travel to the Islamic world, the call to prayer is one of the first clues that the daily lives of Muslims are different from their own. In Christian communities, on

Sunday mornings and on holidays, the faithful are called to worship by the ringing of church bells. In the Islamic world, it is the human voice that summons the believers.

The call to prayer, or *adhan*, is made from the tall structure that is part of most mosques, called a *ma'dhana*, or, in English, minaret. The individuals who call Muslims to prayer are known as *mu'adhdhins*. Traditionally, the mu'adhdhins, or muezzins, made the call from the minaret itself using only their voices. Today, it is common for these men to use microphones along with loudspeakers attached to the upper part of the minaret.

The muezzins deliver the call five times daily in a slow chant. In large towns and cities, these voices form a long wave of sound. For the person visiting the Islamic world for the first time, hearing the call can be a surprising and moving experience.

The call to prayer is rather short. In its opening phrase, *Allahu akhbar* (God is most great), it proclaims the important Islamic belief: God is the supreme being over all things. The call continues: "I bear witness that there is no deity except God," affirming the oneness of God, a central Islamic tenet. The phrase that follows names Muhammad as the prophet of Islam: "I bear witness that Muhammed is the messenger of God." Finally, in two phrases, Muslims are told to "come to prayer" and "come to salvation." The idea behind these phrases is that through prayer Muslims will worship God and, in return, be shown God's favor. The call to prayer ends as it began, with the phrase "Allahu akhbar."

Muslims prepare for each of the daily sessions of prayer with a short ritual of cleansing called the *wudu'*. They wash with plain water at designated areas in the mosques. There are usually wash basins located in mosques for this purpose. At home or at the workplace, Muslims simply use the facilities available.

With the wudu' complete, the Muslim is ready for prayer. Although it is considered best to pray with other Muslims, it is perfectly acceptable to pray alone—at home for example. When Muslims pray together, they do so in a row, side by side. If men and women are together, the women must pray behind or separately from the men. In many parts of the Islamic world, women commonly pray at home and it is the men who use the mosques regularly.

Standing in front of the rows of faithful is a single individual who leads the prayer. In the mosques, the prayer is usually led by a person known as the *imam,* or prayer leader. Outside the mosques, when Muslims pray together they simply choose someone to lead; often this person is an older man, chosen for his piety. The imam and the rows of persons behind him all face in the same direction, toward the holy city of Mecca and the sacred Ka'bah.

The salat consists of spoken phrases and a set of four postures: standing, bowing, prostrating and sitting. These postures are carried out in a regular cycle that every Muslim learns as a child. There is a slightly different cycle of phrases and postures for each of the five daily prayers. It is considered a pious act for Muslims to repeat part or all of a cycle of prayer. The spoken phrases are short, voluntary prayers to God.

The prayer ends each time in the same way. Turning to the left and to the right, each individual wishes the persons beside them peace and the blessings of God. This is one way in which Muslims affirm that they are all members of the same community, and that they share a common belief in the one god.

The second of the pillars of Islam is a short statement known as the *shahadah*, or bearing witness. The content of the shahadah is

■ *Pakistani Muslims gather for worship at the Badshahi Mosque in the northern Pakistani city of Lahore. One of the largest mosques in the world, the Badshahi holds nearly 100,000 worshipers. It was built in the late 17th century by the Mughal dynasty.*

similar to that of the call to prayer in that it proclaims the oneness of God. Most Muslims learn this statement when they are children. It is also the statement that all converts to Islam are required to make at the time of their conversion. This short utterance expresses the most fundamental beliefs of the Islamic faith, and learning and reciting it from the heart constitutes one's symbolic joining of the Islamic community.

Fasting and the Alms

Sawm, or ritual fasting, is the third pillar of Islam. This fast takes place each year during Ramadan, the ninth month of the Islamic calendar. During the fast of Ramadan, which lasts for the entire month, strict restraints are placed upon the daily lives of Muslims. For example, they are not to eat or drink during the daylight hours. When the sun sets at the end of each day, Muslims break the fast, but even then they are expected to eat and drink in moderation. The fast re-sumes the next morning. Traditionally, the beginning of the fast each day takes place when there is enough light in the sky to distinguish between a white and dark thread. Smoking is also forbidden during Ramadan as are sexual relations. Ramadan is meant to be a time of physical abstinence and increased devotion to religious practice.

The fast can be very demanding. It sometimes takes place in the summer when, in much of the Islamic world, the days are long and hot, making it dangerous to go without water. For these reasons, the sick, the elderly, and the very young are not expected to observe the fast. Travelers are also exempt but are expected to make up for the lost days later in the year.

The fast of Ramadan has been criticized by some Muslims because of the demands it makes upon the individual and upon society. Some Muslims argue that it is wasteful to have people observe the fast so closely. They insist that people naturally work more slowly and poorly when they are not eating. Some of these critics say that people should be given the choice of whether or not to fast or that the fast should be shortened in some way.

Against these arguments other Muslims respond that, on the contrary, the fast needs to be carefully observed because Ramadan is the only time when Muslims can fully concentrate on the practice of their faith, while spending less time on the concerns of their everyday lives. It is a time of worship and of contemplation—a time for Muslims to strengthen their ties to family and community.

As is true in every religious community, there are many Muslims who do not closely observe the rituals of their faith. In private, for example, there are Muslims who choose not to fast, just as they often choose not to pray. What is interesting about Ramadan, however, is that in public it is extremely rare to find a Muslim eating or drinking during daylight hours. In many parts of the Islamic world, cafes and restaurants remain closed through much of the day or only serve foreign tourists.

For those who do observe the fast, Ramadan is a spiritual time during which the Muslim concentrates more than ever on religious activities, such as reading the Koran. It is not uncommon for Muslim men to reserve several days of Ramadan for spiritual retreat, when one turns away from the world and dedicates oneself to religious matters.

Ramadan is also a time when Muslims are expected to pay more attention to the hungry, the poor and the deprived. Sharing food with less fortunate neighbors, for example, or donating clothes are ways in which this need is met. The Koran itself speaks of the support that Muslims should give to the needy of their communities. Such acts are also a way to demonstrate one's commitment to the faith.

The fourth pillar of Islam addresses the needs of the poor and the destitute more directly. The *zakat*, or almsgiving, is a kind of religious tax that all Muslims who can afford to are expected to pay at a specified time each year. The money collected is set aside for specific groups of people in the Islamic community including the poor, the sick, the insane and other groups who are unable to fend for themselves. For Muslims, the zakat is not considered charity but rather an important religious obligation. In most of the Islamic world today, the zakat is not enforced by the government; rather, it is expected that Muslims will pay voluntarily. Like the other four pillars, zakat plays an important part in the religious life of Muslims. The Koran states that giving alms is one of the duties that God requires of Muslims.

The zakat is often confused with another act, known as *sadaqah*. This is also the giving of alms but, unlike the zakat, it is an act of charity, not an obligation. Also unlike the zakat, it is not a set amount of money. Following noontime prayer on Friday, the sacred day in Islam, Muslims often practice sadaqah by giving small amounts of change or food to beggars outside the mosques.

The Fifth Pillar: Pilgrimage

The fifth pillar of Islam is one that all Muslims are strongly encouraged to perform at least once in their lives: the pilgrimage to the holy city of Mecca, or, as it is called by Muslims, the *hajj*. Each year, during the twelfth Islamic month of Dhu al-Hijja, Muslims from all over the Islamic world perform the sacred journey. In Mecca, they participate in an elaborate set of rituals during a period of five days. Unlike the other four pillars of Islam, the hajj is not obligatory; only those who have reached maturity and who have the financial resources to pay for the trip while still providing for dependents at home are expected to perform the pilgrimage.

The first act of the pilgrimage is putting on a clean white garment known as an *ihram*. Wearing this garment is obligatory for men, but women are encouraged to wear the clothing that is native to their home countries. Women are required to keep their heads covered for the entire period of the pilgrimage, but men must keep their heads bare. From this point until the end of the hajj, the pilgrims are considered to be in a state of holiness

After their arrival in Mecca, pilgrims set out to perform the rituals of the hajj. Muslims from non-Arabic-speaking regions of the world are often assisted by guides, known as *mutawwifs*, who are employees of the Saudi Arabian government. The guides translate for the pilgrims who do not speak or understand Arabic and assist them in carrying out the rituals.

Some of the rituals are performed at the choice of the individual. These include sessions of prayer and another ritual known as the *tawaf*, which involves walking around the Ka'bah at least seven times. The pilgrims have less choice when it comes to the group rituals, which are the main rituals of the hajj.

The group rituals are carried out in a set order during the five days of the pilgrimage. One such ritual takes place in the small

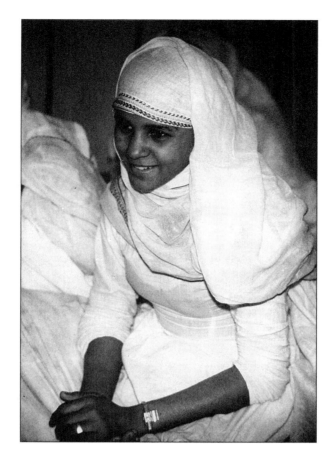

A young Muslim woman on the pilgrimage to Mecca. She is wearing a simple, white garment known as the **ihram.** Male pilgrims are required to wear this garment while women are given a choice. They may wear the ihram or their native costume. Women are required, however, to cover their hair at all times while on the pilgrimage.

town of Mina, just outside of Mecca. There, on a wide plain known as Arafat, pilgrims carry out the *wukuf,* or standing ceremony, in which they are required to be present on the plain from noon to sunset. It is the one occasion during the hajj when all the pilgrims must be together. Tents are erected for the huge crowd, and for this single day of the year the plain of Arafat resembles a very busy town. During these hours, pilgrims are expected to pray quietly. At the center of the plain is a small mountain known as the Mount of Mercy. During this day, pilgrims ascend the mountain, where they ask God to forgive them of their sins. All pilgrims must carry out these rituals at Arafat; failure to do so means the pilgrimage was incomplete and must be repeated in another year.

Although the pilgrimage to Mecca may be a financial burden for some and especially strenuous for the elderly, most devout Muslims yearn to take part in it. For the individual Muslim, the importance of the hajj cannot be overemphasized. In a way, the pilgrimage is a greater version of the salat—the prayer for which Muslims each day face in the direction of Mecca and the Ka'bah. During the pilgrimage, however, the Muslim is actually in Mecca, which is sometimes referred to as the house of God. Thus, in Mecca the pilgrim is in a way one of God's visitors. As the house of God, Mecca is the holiest site in the world for Muslims.

When the five days of the hajj are over, the pilgrims take off the ihram. During the next few days, pilgrims continue to pray and perform at least two more of the tawafs around the Ka'bah. With the second of these, which is called the farewell tawaf, the pilgrimage is then considered complete. Many pilgrims add one last part to their voyage—a visit to Muhammad's tomb, in Medina—so that they may pay their respects to the prophet of Islam.

The pilgrims make their way back to their home countries by plane, bus, ship and train. Upon their arrival they are usually greeted with a joyous welcome by their families and neighbors. The accomplishment of the pilgrimage is a time to celebrate. The pilgrim, after all, has been through one of the most important events in the life of a Muslim. Having made the holy journey to Mecca and the Ka'bah, the pilgrim is now a *hajji*, or, if the pilgrim is a woman, a *hajjah*.

The pilgrimage brings together Muslims from all over the world. It is a time when Muslims of many different backgrounds, speaking different languages and practicing different customs, share a common and intense experience. Ever since Muhammad set out on the first pilgrimage to Mecca, many accounts of the hajj have been written. These descriptions show how moving the experience of the pilgrimage is for Muslims.

The Rituals of the Shi'ah

While all Muslims are expected to carry out the hajj and the other four pillars of Islam to the best of their abilities, the Shi'ah perform additional rituals as well. The focus of the most important of these rituals is the 10th day of the Islamic month of Muharram. On that day in 680 Husayn, the grandson of Muhammad, was killed in battle by Umayyad soldiers. The day is known as Ashura.

The centerpiece of the rituals of Ashura is the elaborate performance known as *ta'ziyah*, or passion play. Performed during Muharram in every Shi'i community, the passion play is a detailed and emotional reenactment of the death of Husayn. While we can think of it as theater, it is quite unlike the plays one might attend in the West. One obvious difference is that audience participation is not only expected, it is encouraged.

On stage, before a captive audience, actors carry out the events of Husayn's death in remarkable detail. More than just his death is portrayed, however. All of the events involving the Shi'i community and its imams in their struggle against the Umayyad and Abbasid caliphs is described and acted out. The climax of the performance is the attack on Husayn and his infant son.

As the story builds to its inevitable climax, emotions both on and off the stage begin to grow. Throughout the performance, members of the audience offer advice to the actors, shout and laugh when the imams are doing well and fall sad when things turn badly for the imams and their followers. These emotions reach a peak with the attack on Husayn. As the Umayyad soldiers close in with their spears and swords, hacking away at the imam and his horse, and when Husayn's head is finally severed, members of the audience weep and shout out curses against the Umayyad soldiers. On occasion, with a particularly vivid performance, audience members have been known to leap on stage and rush at the actors playing the soldiers in order to protect Husayn and his family.

Other ritual events surround the passion play. Frequently, before the play a processional is held in which models of the Ka'bah and the tombs of the imams are carried. Members of the community display ornate banners drawn with scenes of the deaths of the imams and on which are written verses of the Koran and sayings from the imams.

The processions of the ta'ziyah include another event that many non-Shi'ah have found disturbing. In the processions march lines of men, many stripped to the waist, striking themselves

■ *In New Delhi, the capital of India, Shi'i Muslims walk in a ritual procession commemorating the death of Husayn ibn Ali, the grandson of the Prophet Muhammad. Known as the* **ta'ziyah,** *this ritual procession is carried out by Shi'i Muslims on the 10th day of the month of Muharram. Husayn, the third Imam, is highly revered by the Shi'ah.*

across the shoulders or head with knives and chains, while chanting rhythmically the name of Husayn.

For the foreign visitor, these scenes can be shocking. For the Shi'ah, their meaning is clear: Ashura is a time to express deep emotions of pain and anger. In the year 680, the Shi'ah had called on the Imam Husayn to claim his place as leader of the Islamic community. When he finally responded to their call and set out to meet them, they failed to support him. Rather than march out to join him in fighting the hated Umayyad rulers, the Shi'ah stayed home and left Husayn to be slaughtered. It is during Ashura that the Shi'i community expresses guilt over its failure to act and anguish over the death of the beloved Husayn.

Husayn is remembered in another way during Ashura. This is during the *rawda-khani*, or recital of the suffering of the Imam Husayn. An individual or family will invite a group of friends to a private gathering. There a professional reciter will tell the story of Husayn's martyrdom, often in great detail. A skilled reciter will touch his listeners deeply, bringing tears to their eyes and perhaps rousing them to their feet, crying out the name of Husayn. Like the passion play, these can be extremely emotional events.

The Shi'ah honor the imams in other ways. In premodern times, local dynasties could not always guarantee the safety of pilgrims traveling to Mecca. So, for a long time, visitations to the tombs of the imams were seen as an acceptable substitute to the hajj. Today, even though the Shi'ah of Iran, Iraq and other Shi'i areas take part in the pilgrimage to Mecca, it is considered a pious act to visit these tombs, as well as those belonging to lesser members of the Alid family.

The Rituals of the Sufis

Throughout Islamic history, Sunnis and Shi'ah alike have also carried out the rituals of Sufism. By the 14th century, Sufism was so widespread in the Islamic world that it was commonplace for ordinary Muslims to carry out Sufi rituals. The broad term used for these rituals is *dhikr*. In carrying out dhikr, the Sufi repeats the names of God—Muslims believe that God has 99 names—and his attributes. Dhikrs may be carried out in private, where it is usually practiced to compliment prayer, or they may be performed in groups by the Sufi orders. Each of these orders has its own special dhikr developed by the early masters of the order and their students.

In the group dhikrs, some of the orders simply repeat the word Allah over and over again: sometimes in a soft whisper, sometimes in a loud, clear chant. Some orders will do so while

■ **The Names of God**
Among the 99 names of God are: al-Rahman ("The Compassionate"), al-Rahim ("The "Merciful"), al-Aziz ("The Mighty") and al-Khaliq ("The Creator").

sitting calmly. Most prefer to stand, and often the participants will sway from side to side as they utter the dhikr. Other Sufi orders have developed more elaborate rituals where long phrases in praise of God and Muhammad are repeated. Such rituals may include intense physical movement such as dancing or a strong rocking motion of the upper body. Regardless of the form it takes, the goal of the dhikr is nearly always the same: to draw closer to God.

Performing dhikr became a common part of the religious lives of many, if not most, Muslims in the 14th century. In neighborhoods and villages throughout the Islamic world, Muslims met in mosques and Sufi centers to perform dhikr with the other members of their orders. Dhikr would be performed on religious holidays and on other special occasions, such as the prophet Muhammad's birthday.

By this period, another kind of ritual practice was also common. For the ordinary Muslim, the religious world was inhabited not only by God and the prophets, but also by deeply spiritual individuals we might refer to as saints. Among these saints were Sufi masters, holymen and holywomen who were seen in many parts of the Islamic world as possessing *barakah*— a spiritual power given them by God. Barakah enabled them to carry out miraculous acts, such as healing the sick.

The barakah of the saintly individual was believed to live on after the individual's death. It was carried on by the members of the saint's family, and more often it was believed to inhabit the tomb in which the saint was buried. Consequently, visits to the tombs of saints became commonplace. For ordinary Muslims, the goal of such a visit was to be touched by the saint's powers—by the barakah.

A visit to the tomb often involved certain rituals. Visitors would bring small offerings to the saint or the saint's family. Plates of food, small gifts or sums of money were common offerings. They would also touch the tomb of the saint, which would become worn in places where it had been touched often over the years. Prayers might also be performed, or a portion of the Koran read aloud. This writer has witnessed visits by Muslims to the tomb of a local saint in the southern Moroccan city of Marrakech. After reciting a brief Koranic verse or prayer, the visitors then left small rags tied to the bars crisscrossing the windows of the tomb. In this way, the visitors were seeking to win the help of the saint and a small touch of the barakah.

Many in the community, especially religious leaders, scholars and better-educated Muslims, objected strongly to the veneration of the saints. In their view, the teachings of Islam were being corrupted by such practices. Their opinions seem to have led a number of Muslims to stop engaging in these activities, but even today others continue to practice them.

One particularly angry attack on the practice of tomb visits, and on Sufism as a whole, came from a radical movement that appeared in Arabia in the 18th century. Known as the Wahhabi movement, it was able to seize control of much of the Arabian Peninsula in the early 20th century. The state it established bore the name of a large tribal clan that supported the movement: the Sa'ud clan. This was the creation of what we know today as Saudi Arabia. One of the first measures taken by the new state was the destruction of the tombs of the Sufi masters and the other saints. The veneration of the saints was denounced. As a result, today Saudi Arabia is one of the few areas of the Islamic world where Sufism is completely absent.

CHAPTER 7

The Patterns
of Islamic Life

*L*ife is as varied in the Islamic world as it is in other, non-Islamic parts of the globe. In small Muslim villages in Egypt or Bangladesh, farmers work the fields, tend their crops and orchards and raise their goats, sheep and cows. In the larger Muslim cities and towns—such as Rabat, Damascus or Djakarta—shopping and business districts bustle with traffic and pedestrians. In the neighborhoods of the middle class and rich, streets and yards are clean, and the houses are well-kept. In poor neighborhoods, streets and buildings are run-down, sidewalks are broken and hunger and crime pose daily problems. In these areas, as in most parts of the world where the poor live and work, people struggle to provide for themselves and their families.

As in non-Muslim countries, the Muslim household begins the workday with a flurry of activity as children are fed and readied for school, and the father prepares for work. Although the man of a Muslim household is almost always the main wage earner, this is slowly changing as more women become educated and become part of the workforce. Women who stay home

spend their days tending to the needs of children, shopping and maintaining the home.

Evenings are often a time for families to eat together, and after dinner many households in the Islamic world, as is common elsewhere, turn to the television for entertainment. On weekends and holidays, Muslims enjoy various forms of recreation—from sports to picnics to fairs—depending partly on the time of year and the weather. As in most parts of the world, with the exception of the United States, soccer is the sport of choice in most Islamic countries.

Certain patterns of behavior however are unique to the lives of Muslims, including such ritual practices as the pilgrimage to Mecca and the fast of Ramadan. Although many other customs and habits are common throughout the Islamic world, it would be wrong to think that all Muslims live in the same way.

Muslim lives are shaped not only by Islamic norms and activities, but also by the customs and habits that are native to each area of the Islamic world. For this reason, Muslims in Indonesia or Senegal do not live in exactly the same way that Muslims in China, Afghanistan or Morocco do. Everywhere, Muslims have adapted Islamic norms and values to local customs and beliefs.

The variety of languages that Muslims speak is an example of the important differences amongst Muslims. Arabic, as the language of the Koran, has a special status among Muslims and is almost always used when the Koran is recited. Scholars and students of Islam throughout the world learn to read and write Arabic; many come to al-Azhar and other universities in Arab countries to do so. The vast majority of Muslims, however, speak no Arabic other than a handful of verses from the Koran. In Pakistan, Urdu is the common language of Muslims; in Turkey and parts of Central Asia, it is Turkish; and in Iran, Farsi is spoken on a daily basis. Other languages are spoken in other regions of the Islamic world. This does not mean, however, that the Koran cannot be understood by these Muslims. In each non-Arabic-speaking region, local languages are used in religious classes and in sermons to teach the Koran and Hadith. The Koran is also made available in translation.

Although their way of life may vary greatly from region to region and country to country, depending on local customs and habits, most Muslims have some patterns of life in common.

The Friday Prayer

In Islam, Friday is the one day of the week set aside for special religious observances. Every Friday, Muslims attend a special session of worship that takes place at noon. In many areas of the Islamic world, mosques are so crowded on Fridays that people pray outside on long mats provided by the mosques. In Cairo, for example, it is not unusual to find some side streets closed to traffic on Friday mornings. Long straw mats are rolled out on these streets to accommodate the faithful.

Unlike Sunday in the Christian world, Friday is not considered an official day of rest by Muslims. Still, it has become traditional in many Islamic countries for businesses to close around noon so that business owners and employees may attend the Friday prayer. In areas that cater to tourists, shops and restaurants may remain open through the day. Even there, many Muslims will take the afternoon off to be with family and friends.

What makes the Friday prayer session special is the sermon given by the imam or by another individual chosen for their knowledge of the Koran. The sermon is known as the *khutbah*, and it is made up of two parts: the preacher begins with a recitation of a portion of the Koran and then proceeds to the sermon. Most often, the subject of the sermon is the Koranic passage itself. The preacher will explain the passage in simple language and discuss how that portion of the sacred book relates to the lives of his listeners. During the month of Ramadan, for example, the preacher will discuss how fasting is an important duty required of the Muslim.

While most often the preacher will address religious matters, he may use the Friday sermon to talk of other subjects as well. For example, he may comment on social problems, such as poverty, crime and drug abuse; in times of war he may urge his listeners to support the government against its enemies, or he may call on the government to find a peaceful solution. In many parts of the Islamic world, the Friday sermon given by a leading preacher will be broadcast over the radio or be shown on television, reaching millions of people.

The Mosques

Not all mosques are used for the Friday sermon. Most mosques are fairly small and are generally used by residents of the immediate neighborhood. The small, local mosque is known as a masjid, or place of prostration. For the Friday prayer session, a larger and more centrally located mosque, or *jami'*, is used. In small towns and villages, only one such mosque might exist, whereas in the larger cities, a small number of these larger mosques are present in different areas of the city.

Over the course of Islamic history, several of these large Friday mosques became important educational centers. Perhaps the most renowned of all is the university of al-Azhar in the historical center of Cairo. For centuries, it has attracted students and scholars from all parts of the Islamic world: Students from the Sudan or Nigeria interact with those from as far away as Malaysia and Pakistan. For much of its history, al-Azhar was strictly a religious center where Muslims could study the Koran and Hadith and delve into other areas of Islamic education. Today, al-Azhar is a major university, offering courses in a range of fields in addition to the religious subjects it has traditionally offered.

All mosques, whether small or large, have certain similar features. Most, if not all, provide running water so that those coming to pray can carry out the wudu', or ritual cleansing, that is expected of all Muslims before prayer. All have large, clear central areas where those in prayer can line up in rows for the performance of worship. And all have what is known as the *mihrab*. Muslims must pray in the direction of Mecca, and in order to indicate the direction of the holy city, a niche is built into the appropriate wall. This niche is the mihrab, while the direction of Mecca is known as the *qiblah*. The Koran itself calls on Muslims to "turn their faces" in the direction of Mecca and the Ka'bah in prayer.

Many mosques also have a *minbar*—the pulpit from which the preacher gives the Friday sermon. In some mosques, the minbar may only be a raised platform, whereas in many others it is a set of stairs leading to a small stage closed in by a railing. It can be quite an elaborate structure. In the mosque of Ibn Tulun in Cairo, one of the oldest mosques in the world, the minbar is built of dark brown wooden panels carved in wonderful and very intricate designs.

Christian churches are usually decorated with stained glass, paintings and statues, but mosques, almost without exception, are not. Instead, they are decorated with inscriptions of the Koran. These can cover the walls and ceilings of the mosque, including the inside of the dome that sits atop many mosques. These inscriptions are but one example of the dominant art form in Islamic culture: calligraphy.

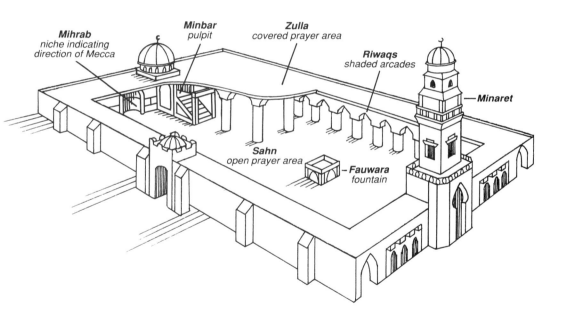

Mihrab
niche indicating
direction of Mecca

Minbar
pulpit

Zulla
covered prayer area

Riwaqs
shaded arcades

Minaret

Sahn
open prayer area

Fauwara
fountain

Annual Festivals

The larger mosques, such as al-Azhar, are commonly located in busy commercial areas. From Islam's early history, merchants have been drawn to the mosques because they are centers of so

■ *In Algiers, the capital of Algeria, women enter a small mosque. Before entering the mosque, Muslims remove their shoes, placing them in a designated area near the entrance. Mosques range greatly in size, from the enormous "communal" mosques found in many urban centers, to those much smaller in size found in villages and local neighborhoods.*

much activity, religious and otherwise. As a result, one finds in Islamic cities large numbers of shops, bookstores and small restaurants lining the streets and alleys that circle these mosques. With mosque and marketplace side by side, these areas are usually among the busiest and most congested parts of town. They become especially crowded during religious holidays and other special occasions, such as the month-long fast of Ramadan.

Although Ramadan is considered a duty that Muslims are expected to take quite seriously, and the physical demands of the fast are taxing, Ramadan also has its lighter side. In most parts of the Islamic world, it brings a marked change in the pace of life. Activity during the daylight hours slows considerably; people become quieter, less active and sometimes more moody than they normally are. With the end of the day, however, the fast is broken, and it is expected that Muslims will break the fast with prayer and a short meal known as the *iftar*. In some parts of the Islamic world, such as Morocco, the meal may consist of a thick soup with bread and fruit.

Following the break of the fast, things grow festive. In the towns and cities of the Middle East, as well as other areas of the Islamic world, it is customary for Muslims to go out after the iftar. They visit with family and friends or simply stroll. Shopping districts often remain quite busy as shops and restaurants stay open. In cafes, people sip tea and fruit drinks and engage in lively conversation. In Cairo, near the al-Azhar mosque, a book fair is held during Ramadan. And nearby, beneath large canvas tents, members of Sufi groups recite the Koran and perform their dhikrs. These rituals attract many onlookers, including tourists.

The high point of Ramadan comes toward the very end of the month. On the evening of the 27th day, Muslims celebrate what is known as the Night of Power. According to Islamic tradition, it was on this night, in 610, that Muhammad first received the revelation of the Koran. In at least one place in the Islamic world— Marrakech, Morocco—the evening is a noisy one as young men race through the streets exploding fireworks. Another important occasion comes with the end of Ramadan. On the first day of the next month, Shawwal, Muslims celebrate a special and long-awaited holiday known as the Feast of Fast Breaking, or *Eid al-Fitr*. For three days, Muslims gather with family and friends for long meals, the sharing of gifts and, often, religious devotion. In many Islamic countries, the Eid is a national holiday. Those who are abroad for work or study travel home to be with family. For many Muslims, it is a time to celebrate the renewed commitment to their faith and to offer thanks to God for having seen them through the long fast.

Another important celebration of the year comes during the month of pilgrimage, Dhu al-Hijjah. One of the rituals carried out toward the end of the pilgrimage in Mecca is the sacrifice of animals, usually sheep, goats or camels. In Mecca, while some of the meat is eaten by the pilgrims, much of it is distributed to the poor. The Saudi Arabian government is also looking for ways to preserve the meat for export. In the rest of the Islamic world, a similar sacrifice is made by each household or neighborhood. In the weeks leading up to this celebration, known as *Eid al-Adha*, or the Feast of Sacrifice, it is quite common to see great numbers of sheep and goats, sometimes in unexpected places. This writer has seen adult sheep being transported in the back seats of taxis and tied in bundles on top of buses, and feeding on the terraces of apartment buildings and in the back rooms of shops.

Mawlids

For many Muslims, though certainly not all, the mawlid is another occasion of celebration. It is a festival marking the birthday of a saint or some other revered person of the past. No mawlid is more widely observed than that of Muhammad. Known as the *mawlid al-nabi* and held every year during Rabia al-Awwal, the third Islamic month, it signals the deep veneration felt by Muslims for Muhammad.

The mawlid al-nabi is celebrated in a variety of ways. Special prayers are said in Muhammad's honor, for example, and often Sufi groups will hold public dhikrs in which his name is praised. In large cities and towns, centrally located areas are decorated with lights and banners. There, people congregate to eat sweets, meet friends and family, spend money at small games booths and relax.

The calendar year is marked by other mawlids as well, most often held in honor of saints. These celebrations, known in some areas as *musims*, can vary in size and importance. A saint may be venerated in only a particular town or even neighborhood, in which case the festival is attended by a limited number of people. Other mawlids, however, can attract Muslims, not to speak of tourists, from all over a particular nation or even region of the Islamic world. Though sometimes noisy and terribly crowded, they can be great fun.

In Morocco, the site of one annual celebration is the small town of Mulay Idris. Located near the northern city of Meknes, the town features an elaborate shrine, in which is located the tomb of Mulay Idris, after whom the town is named. Sometimes referred to as the national saint of Morocco, Mulay Idris was the founder of the first Islamic dynasty in Morocco in the late 8th century. Topped by a beautiful green dome, the shrine was built in the latter part of the 15th century. Since that time, the festival in honor of Mulay Idris has drawn large numbers of people from all over Morocco and remains a popular event to the present day.

In sheer numbers, perhaps no mawlid is larger than that of Ahmad al-Badawi, held each fall in the Egyptian town of Tanta. It is an enormously popular event—one that many Egyptians are reluctant to miss. The celebrations in Mulay Idris and for al-Badawi in Tanta share a number of features. At both events, people gather to be touched by the barakah of the saint. Those who can, try to touch the tomb of the saint while murmuring prayers

---

■ Islamic Days of Observance

Id al-Adha (known also as *Id al-Kabir*)—This is the festival of sacrifice held throughout the Islamic world on the tenth day of the month of Dhu al-Hijja. The sacrifice is an important element of the pilgrimage to Mecca, the Hajj.

Id al-Fitr (known also as *Id al-Saghir*)—Held on the first day of the month of Shawwal, this is the feast celebrating the end of Ramadan. This is a particularly joyful event for Muslims.

Mawlid al-Nabi—The birthday of the Prophet Muhammad, held on the twelfth day of the month of Rabia I. A particularly popular event. Nabi, or "prophet," is one of the titles given to Muhammad. The Shi'ah celebrate his birthday on the seventeenth day of that month, which is also the birthday of Ja'far al-Sadiq, the Sixth Imam.

Ashura—During the first ten days of the month of Muharram, the Shi'i community commemorates the suffering and death of Imam Husayn, the Prophet's grandson and the Third Imam. These events reach their peak on the tenth day, which is known as Ashura.

The Shi'ah also commemorate the birthdays of each of the Imams. In Iran, which has a Twelver Shi'i majority, each of these twelve birthdays is considered a national holiday. For example, the first of their Imams, Ali ibn Abi Talib, is believed to have been born on the thirteenth day of the month of Rajab.

or repeating the name of Mulay Idris or al-Badawi. In the barakah, it is believed, lies the power to bring one good luck, strength, good health or even success in school or in a business deal.

These celebrations are usually very festive. Sufi groups gather to hold their dhikrs and attract new members. Processions, organized by Sufis and other groups as well, take place. During these processions, banners are displayed, and often the leader of the Sufi order is brought out on horseback for all to see. Attracted by the large crowds, musicians, story-tellers, traveling merchants and preachers come to practice their skills and earn money. Tents, in which everything from food to clothes to spices and charms are sold, are erected in any clear area. Both events last for days, and many of those in attendance spend nights wherever they can—be it in a mosque, on the floors of houses and shops or in a quiet area on the ground.

Feast days, mawlids and other such occasions are celebrated throughout the Islamic world. If one turns from these noisier, more public events to the quieter world of Muslim family life, one discovers patterns that are much more private but no less a part of the lives of Muslims the world over.

Muslim Childhood

Several events mark the first years of a Muslim child's life. Around the time of birth, the infant is given a Muslim name. It is common, at least within devout Muslim families, to use the names of highly revered figures of Islamic history.

Muhammad is, as one might expect, the most popular name of all for male children. Others include Umar, after one the first caliphs; and Ali, after Ali ibn Abi Talib. The names Hasan and Husayn are popular as well, since these were the names of Muhammad's grandsons both of whom, it is believed, he loved dearly. Since they were also the first of the Imams, their names are particularly popular among the Shi'ah. Often, males are also given names that are formed from one the names of God, such as Abd Allah (servant of God) or Abd al-Rahman (servant of the All-Merciful).

Female children, similarly, are named after Muhammad's wives and other important and well-known women in early

Islamic history. Khadijah, the name of Muhammad's first wife; Fatimah, the name of one of his daughters; and Aishah, the name of another of Muhammad's wives, are all popular names.

As soon as Muslim children begin to speak, they are taught common religious phrases. Then, short passages from the Koran are learned. One phrase taught to youngsters is *bismillah al-rahman al-rahim*, which means "in the name of God, the Merciful, the Compassionate." It is a set of words used by Muslims throughout their lives, in a variety of situations—before meals, when stepping into a room or onto a bus, when entering a mosque. The phrase gains its importance from the fact that each chapter, or surah, of the Koran begins with these words.

■ *A school in a rural area of Egypt. Many Muslim children, particularly in Arabic-speaking countries, begin their education in small centers in which they learn to read and write by reciting and copying out portions of the Koran. Many then go on to government-run schools such as the one pictured here.*

The Koran is where formal education begins for many Muslim children. In the first year of school or in small centers, known as *kuttabs*, children learn to read by reciting verses from the Koran. In this way, they learn not only to read, but also to recognize the central teachings of their faith. One of the first parts of the Koran learned by all Muslim children is the first surah: the *Surat al-Fatihah*.

For Muslim boys, an event that happens early in their lives is circumcision. In some Muslim areas, this takes place around the age of 10. In other areas, it is not the age that matters, but when the boy is able to recite the entire Koran aloud for the first time. Although the operation itself is usually over in minutes, the occasion is often celebrated in various ways. In parts of Morocco, for example, it is customary for those families that can afford to rent a horse to have the boy paraded around the neighborhood on horseback.

In some parts of the Muslim world, girls and young women may undergo a ritual called female circumcision, or *clitoridectomy*. This operation, which ranges in degree from a small incision to the removal of the clitoris, is carried out in much of Africa. Many Muslims there consider it necessary to preserve the girl's purity and to make her marriageable, believing it to be a religious duty. The operation can have serious health consequences for the young woman, which may include death, either at the time of the surgery or later, in childbirth. In recent years, it has been banned in Egypt, and there is pressure from world health organizations on other governments of the area to follow Egypt's example. Many Islamic scholars now find that the practice has no basis in the Koran but has come into Islam from pre-Islamic customs. However, it remains a deeply rooted practice that will take many years of education to change.

Marriage

Muslims are encouraged to marry and to bear children. In many parts of the Islamic world, as in the non-Islamic world, it has been customary for marriages to be arranged by parents or guardians. This practice is changing, and in urban areas and among the educated classes, a young woman commonly has at least a say in whom she marries. Young men and women may see each other in university classes or at family gatherings, but dating remains rare in the Islamic world. In many regions, for an unmarried couple to be seen together in public alone is still considered behavior that brings shame on both of their families.

Marriage between two people, according to Islamic law, is settled with a contract, in which the rights and duties of both the man and woman are laid out and agreed on by both persons. In many parts of the Islamic world, marriage is seen as the uniting of two families rather than two individuals. Most often, the ceremony itself is rather simple and quiet.

However, for the celebrations that follow, families often spend large sums of money on food, clothes, and gifts. The lavishness of the celebrations depends on the wealth of the families involved and even the poorest families will borrow money in order to stage a proper wedding. Usually, these will be held in the home or just outside the home of one of the two families. They can last throughout the night or even longer. They are often community events, in which an entire village or neighborhood will be invited to join in the celebration. Very often, men and women celebrate at the same time but in separate buildings or areas.

An issue that has been discussed a great deal within the Islamic community is whether or not men should marry more than one wife. This practice, known as polygyny (which is only slightly different from polygamy), seems to have been present in pre-Islamic Arabia, and it is known that Muhammad himself had a number of wives by the end of his life. The Koran states that men may marry up to four wives but only if they can treat each of them equally and fairly (4:3). Since the rise of Islam, polygyny has been a standard practice but scholars are uncertain as to how widespread it has been. Today the practice is the subject of much argument. There are those who say that the practice should be banned because it is impossible to treat more than one wife equally. Many Muslims—both men and women—argue that it is also a form of great discrimination against women and so should be abolished. They point to another verse in the Koran: "You will not be able to treat your wives equally, no matter how hard you try." The practice may still exist today in isolated parts of the Islamic world, but it is extremely rare.

Food and Death

In addition to a discussion of marriage, the Koran provides guidelines for other aspects of the Muslim's personal life, including eating and drinking habits. Muslims are forbidden to consume certain kinds of food and drink. Pork, for example, is forbidden as is the eating of any meat from an animal that has died of natural causes. Muslims may only eat from an animal that has been slaughtered properly, which means that its blood has been drained as much as possible after the slaughter. The drinking of alcohol is also strictly forbidden. The Koran mentions wine specifically, but it is believed that this really meant all substances containing alcohol. This includes cooking wine, and for many Muslims the ban includes any medicines that have alcohol in them.

In many countries of the Islamic world, however, alcoholic beverages are sold and consumed. Some of these countries, such as Algeria, Morocco, and Egypt, have their own national beer and wine companies. In bars and restaurants, beer and wine are sold, although one usually sees only non-Muslim tourists ordering such drinks. The presence and use of these substances has created a great deal of debate, with devout Muslims and religious leaders calling for the banning of the sale and manufacture of all alcoholic beverages. On occasion, bars and hotels have been raided by Muslim activists, who proceed to smash bottles of alcohol and even burn bars to the ground. In some urban areas— Cairo and Casablanca, for example—alcoholism has been recognized as a social problem.

As in every faith, death is marked in Islam with solemn rituals. The last hours of a dying Muslim's life are passed with a recitation of the Koran. The 36th surah of the Koran, entitled *Ya Sin*, is concerned with death and God's judgment, so it is considered the most appropriate part of the Koran to read. A family member or the local imam recites this surah out loud both to comfort the dying person and to prepare that person for the coming judgment. The last three verses of Ya Sin remind the listener of God's power:

> *Is not He, who created the heavens and earth, able to*
> *create the like of them? Yes, surely, He is the Creator*
> *and the All-Knowing. His command, when He desires*

a thing, is to say to it: 'Be!,' and it is. So glory to Him
in whose hand is power over everything. Unto Him
you shall be returned.   (36.81-83)

Following the person's death, a prescribed set of rituals is performed. The body is first carefully washed and prepared for burial by being wrapped in a clean white cloth. Then a funeral service is performed, sometimes in a mosque, often simply at home. The service is often led by the local imam. Following this service the body is then taken to the grave site. It is not required for the corpse to be placed in a coffin. Muslims do not spend a great deal of money on either the burial preparations or the burial itself. The deceased is buried quickly, usually the morning following the death.

The body, carried either in a casket or simply upon a funeral bier, is then carried in a procession of family and friends to the burial site. The procession of a well-known individual will draw large numbers of people, many of whom may join along the way to the graveyard. In 1970, Cairo was the scene of probably the largest single funeral procession in history. Gamal Abd al-Nasir, perhaps the greatest and most respected Arab leader of this century, died of a heart attack in September of that year. His funeral is said to have attracted more than 4 million people, not only from Egypt but also from across the Arabic-speaking world and beyond.

Like the funeral service, a Muslim's burial site is very simple. When the body is placed in the ground, care is taken to see that the head is facing in the direction of Mecca. If the body is in a coffin, usually it is marked to indicate the place of the head. Pious words are then said over the grave, and then there is a recitation of the *Surat al-Fatihah*: the first surah of the Koran. The recitation of this surah symbolizes that the life that has just ended was that of a Muslim. Because Muslims learn the surah early in life, often as one of their first lessons in school, and use it frequently over the course of their lives on all sorts of occasions, it is fitting that at the end of their lives the surah is recited for them this last time.

CHAPTER **8**

Islam
and the
Modern World

By the 18th century, the Islamic community had changed considerably from those first years in Medina, when a small group of Muslims joined Muhammad in establishing the first Islamic settlement. With the number of Muslims now in the millions, the community stretched from the Atlantic coast of Morocco to the many islands of Indonesia. Islam had truly become a world religion.

Over the course of 1200 years, Muslims had faced many serious challenges, from the hostility of the Meccans in the early 7th century to the invasion of the Mongols in the middle of the 13th century. In the 18th century, the Islamic community found itself at the beginning of a new and even more difficult period of history. For at least 200 years, three empires— Mughal, Safavid, and Ottoman—had controlled much of the Islamic world. With their centralized forms of government and strong armies, they had brought stability to the lands of Islam. With stability had also come trade, which meant greater prosperity for all three empires. But all of this came to an end as political and economic strength gave way to decline. The Safavids fell from power in the 18th

century, then the Mughal dynasty crumbled in the 19th century.
The Ottomans would survive into the early 20th century but with
their strength greatly diminished.

The Challenge of the Future

As these empires collapsed, the Islamic world faced an uncertain future. In many regions, local groups fought for political
control. As these conflicts raged on, the stability once provided by
the three empires gave way to social and political upheaval. Faced
with the decline of Muslim power and wealth, many felt deeply
pessimistic. In their minds, Islam had lost the vitality and strength
that had once driven Muslims to establish a world empire. To
many it looked as if Islamic society was on the verge of collapse.

Others felt differently. As the 18th century progressed, individuals and groups appeared determined to see the Islamic community regain its unity and strength. Muslims of different regions
of the Islamic world argued that the decline of Islam could be
stopped. What was needed, they said, was a new commitment on
the part of Muslims to the principles and practices of Islam, as
contained in the Shari'ah. They claimed that too many Muslims
held beliefs and rituals that had little to do with the true religion.
In carrying out such rituals, Muslims were only harming Islam,
and it was time to rid the community of these practices and ideas.
The reformers especially opposed the veneration of the saints and
the questionable practices of many Sufi orders. They argued that
to believe in the magical powers of the saints was a violation of the
most fundamental Islamic belief—the absolute oneness of God.

These Muslims were also critical of the Sufi orders. Many of
the Sufis, they said, encouraged and participated in the veneration
of the saints. They also carried out other unacceptable practices,
such as including wild music and dancing in their rituals. Some of
the reformers called for an end to Sufi practices; others said that
Sufism should be reformed but not eliminated.

Those who pushed for reform and change within Islam were
also critical of many of the religious scholars, or ulama. Traditionally, the ulama were in charge of religious education and handing
down legal opinions. The critics argued that the ulama were too
conservative in their teachings and legal rulings. The problem,

they said, was that the ulama looked too much to the past. Their ideas on law and religion were simply copied from past generations of ulama. While these opinions might have been useful once, they were no longer relevant to the concerns of modern Islamic society. Islam was in a new age, and there were new problems that needed to be solved that the earlier generations of ulama did not have to face.

A New Islam

The new reformers argued that the time had come to put Islam and Islamic society back on the right path. This meant ridding Islam of non-Islamic practices; it meant following the duties and regulations of the Shari'ah more closely; and it meant dealing with the new problems of society in creative ways. For many of these Muslims, the model of action was Muhammad, whom they felt had reformed the society of his day. They sought to follow his example by bringing change to their own societies so that Muslims could face the challenges of the modern world with energy and creativity.

Reform movements appeared in different areas of the Islamic world during the 18th and 19th centuries. Perhaps the earliest was the Wahhabi movement, which appeared in north-ern Arabia in the mid 18th century. Ibn Abd al-Wahhab, a conservative preacher who had studied law and theology in Mecca and Damascus, was then teaching his ideas in Arabia. He preached that Islamic society was being corrupted from within by non-Islamic ideas and practices. Particularly opposed to Sufism and the worship of the saints, he argued fiercely that Muslims should seek guidance from only the Koran and Hadith. He reminded people that the only true model for Islamic society was the one led by Muhammad—a community that had followed the true Islamic way of life, which too many modern Muslims had forgotten or abandoned.

The Wahhabi movement caught the attention and acceptance of a tribal leader named Ibn Saud. Strengthened by this tribe's fighters, the movement conquered much of the Arabian Peninsula, including Mecca in 1803. A small state was created and named after Ibn Saud. In Mecca and Medina, the Wahhabis destroyed the tombs of saints and Sufi centers. They also

> ### ■ Islah and Tajdid
> Two terms that were used a great deal by the reformers of the 18th and 19th century were **islah** ("reform") and **tajdid** ("renewal"). In their view, reform and renewal were required if Islam was to be a vital force in the world.

desecrated the tomb of Muhammad and the tombs of some of his closest followers. For the Wahhabis, it was outrageous that Muslims visited these tombs in search of miracles, when such practices were not, in their view, acceptable to Islam.

At the start of the 19th century, the Wahhabi state was destroyed by an invasion from Egypt. For roughly a century, the Saud family lived in an area in central Arabia, only to reconquer Arabia again in the early 20th century. This was the creation of the modern nation we know as Saudi Arabia.

Another reformer of the 18th century was Uthman Don Fodio (d. 1817), a West African scholar from the area of present-day Nigeria. Trained in Islamic law and theology, he traveled from town to town preaching his ideas of reform. He was critical of the rulers of his region, whom he felt ignored the principles of Islamic law and religion. He accused them of being unjust and tyrannical and of allowing the local population to carry out activities that were contrary to the teachings of Islam, such as rituals involving magic. He preached the need to return to Islamic principles as they were contained in the Shari'ah and to reject all behavior that violated these principles.

Don Fodio was also critical of Muslims who mixed the rituals and beliefs of Islam with practices of other, local religions. Through much of Africa, it was common to find Muslims who continued to use non-Islamic practices alongside the rituals of Islam, or even to mix them together in the same rituals. For Don Fodio, and other reformers of his time, there was no place in Islam for these other practices and beliefs.

This anger over the use of non-Islamic rituals was shared by Shah Wali Allah (d. 1762)—an Indian scholar. Educated in Mecca, and the member of one of the largest Sufi orders of the time, the Naqshbandiyah order, he lived in India during the decline of the Mughal state. He feared that the Islamic society would also decline and felt that only a return to the true ideals of Islam could revitalize his society. Wali Allah was aware that many Muslims in India carried out practices of other religions as well as those of Islam. He was particularly concerned with those who mixed Hindu and Islamic beliefs and practices. It was time, he said, to purify Islam and to make it strong again.

Wali Allah was a Sufi himself and unlike the Wahhabis, he did not call for a ban on Sufism. Rather, he taught that Sufism was acceptable, even necessary, as long as Sufis stayed true to Islam. This meant abiding by the Koran and Hadith and getting rid of questionable beliefs. Sufism, he said, could be an important part of Muslim worship but only if it followed Islamic teachings.

Wali Allah, Don Fodio and others like them promoted a second important belief as well: That the revitalization of Islam might require Muslims to wage *jihad*: or, striving on behalf of Islam. This meant an individual struggle on the part of each Muslim to remain true to the principles of Islam. It also meant armed struggle in the defense of Islam when this was necessary. In 1804, Don Fodio felt the time for jihad had come. Local rulers had passed laws restricting the practices of the Muslim population. In response, Don Fodio declared jihad and gathered an army of followers around him. In a series of wars, his army conquered a large region of West Africa and established the Sokoto state. Run according to Islamic law, this small state survived for roughly a century until 1905.

The spirit of reform and jihad spread throughout the Islamic world during the 18th and into the 19th centuries. In Cyrenaica, part of what is today Libya, the Sanusiyah order arose to establish a strong tribal coalition that would, in the mid 20th century, help the Sanusiyah rise to power. Muhammad ibn Ali al-Sanusi, the founder of the Sanusiyah order, was another outspoken reformer. Like others before him, he called for the purification of Islam and, more specifically, of Sufism. He also expressed the need for jihad in order to bring unity and strength to the faith. His teachings brought together the tribes of the rural areas in which he and his followers preached.

By the late 19th century, these reform movements had influenced many Muslim thinkers and activists, but they had focused on the internal problems of Islamic society. For the Muslim activists of this period that approach was no longer enough. In addition to its internal problems, Muslim society faced a growing threat from outside its boundaries: the increasing military and political power of Europe.

The Threat of Europe

As the countries of Europe grew richer, they began to cast a greedy eye on the regions of the Middle East, Asia, and Africa. By the start of the 19th century, wide regions of the Islamic world had fallen into the hands of European states. To many Muslims, Islam itself was under attack.

In the 19th century, Russia seized a vast area of Central Asia where the population was primarily Muslim, as it is today. The Dutch moved to seize Indonesia and parts of Malaysia. By 1911, they controlled both areas. It was the British and the French, however, who would rule over the largest parts of the Islamic world. By the early 19th century, Britain controlled most of the Indian Peninsula and areas further east in Southeast Asia. By the end of the century, they had added Egypt and the Sudan to their empire. In the 1820s, the French began sending troops against the regions of North Africa. Algeria fell first, around 1830, followed by Tunisia in 1881 and Morocco in 1912. Italy invaded the remaining area of North Africa (what is today Libya) in 1911.

The Ottomans were defeated and driven out of the Arab regions of the Middle East by Great Britain and by a widespread Arab revolt in northern Arabia and Syria during World War I. Britain had promised to help the Arab regions achieve independence, but instead, Britain and France decided in 1916 to carve up the Middle East between themselves. Britain seized a wide band of territory that included Palestine, Jordan, and Iraq, while the French took over the area that would later become Syria and Lebanon.

As a result, by the early 20th century, the vast majority of the lands of Islam were European colonial states. In these regions, Muslims now had very limited control over their political and economic lives. As the presence of the Europeans became greater, it became clear that Muslims would have to accept drastic changes in their societies.

The Penetration of the West

Colonial powers brought enormous changes to the lands they dominated. First, they established European-style schools throughout the Islamic world. Students there learned European political and economic ideas as well as European approaches to science and technology. As students graduated and entered the labor market, they carried these ideas into society at large. Second, the colonial powers changed economic and business practices in Muslim regions. Commerce and production now benefited the Europeans rather than the local regions. Traditional merchants were forced out of business, while a new generation of traders with strong ties to European trade arose.

Over time, as those schooled in European ways gained wealth and power, they spread their practices to wider groups. Many Muslims were ready to accept the new ideas; others were suspicious of the changes being introduced into Islamic society. But regardless of what values they held, most Muslims agreed that the Islamic world was in crisis. They faced disturbing questions: How were Muslims to react to the presence of the Europeans? What values and ideas would Muslims carry into the future? At stake was the future of Islam and Islamic society.

■ *The University of the Punjab in Lahore, Pakistan. In the 19th and 20th centuries, many areas of the Islamic world fell under the rule of European colonial powers. The European powers helped establish Western-style schools and universities which became increasingly popular among the middle and upper classes of these Muslim regions.*

The conservative ulama and their supporters called for a rejection of European values and institutions. They called on Muslims to commit themselves more fully to the principles of Islam. Only then, they argued, would the Islamic community regain its unity and be able to compete with European states.

Other Muslims felt this attitude was too conservative. They agreed that it was important to defend Islam. But they argued that if the Islamic world were to compete with the European states, it would have to adapt. They accused the ulama of living in the past and of not recognizing that Islamic law and education had to be reshaped if Muslims were to meet the challenges of the modern world. These critics felt that rather than reject everything European, Muslims should use those ideas and institutions from Europe that could help to revitalize Islamic society.

Reformers of Islam

Many of the reform-minded Muslims took a strong interest in Western scientific ideas. They proposed that such ideas be incorporated into Islamic education. Science would thus open the way in the Islamic world to new military and scientific technologies, which would benefit the society as a whole.

Such reformers as Jamal al-Din al-Afghani (d. 1897), Muhammad Abduh (d. 1905), and Rashid Rida (d.1935), looked for ways to adapt Islam to modern times. In Islam, they argued, lay all of the principles necessary to create a modern Islamic world. They agreed that the rituals of Islam and the guidance of the Shari'ah were essential to Muslim life, but they believed that if the Shari'ah was to deal with the problems of modern Islamic society, it would have to be updated. This meant using the main principles of the Shari'ah to create a modern code of rules and laws. Only a new and revitalized Shari'ah, they said, could put Islamic society back on its feet.

Many of these ideas were shared by two other leading Muslim thinkers of the late 19th and early 20th centuries: Sayyid Ahmad Khan (d. 1898), and later, Muhammad Iqbal (d.1938). Iqbal, a lawyer, admired European democracy and parliamentary government. He did not believe, however, that Muslims needed to borrow these ideas from Europe. Like al-Afghani, he felt that these ideas were contained in the principles of the Shari'ah and that Muslims needed only to reinterpret the Shari'ah to reveal them.

Although their writings would influence generations after them, Abduh, Iqbal, and the others never became politically powerful. For one thing, their thinking attracted mostly students and intellectuals—not the broad population of Muslims. In addition, they faced opposition from other Muslim thinkers. On one side, the conservative ulama rejected the use of all European ideas and institutions, believing that such ideas were outside Islam. On the other side, a new generation of Muslims felt comfortable with European political and economic ideas. This second group included those who embraced the idea of nationalism—the notion that a people should govern themselves and determine their own future without influence from foreign powers. It was an idea that would change the face of the Islamic world over the course of the twentieth century.

The Idea of Nationalism

Nationalist ideas were spread by Muslim students who had been educated in European schools. These included both schools that had been established in Muslim regions and the universities in Europe itself at which Muslim youth studied. As new generations of Muslim students graduated, the idea of nationalism caught on throughout the Islamic world.

The concept of nationalism gave rise to a number of political movements, all aimed at ending European colonialism. Their leaders usually included young Western-educated lawyers, journalists, and engineers. Earlier reformers had been committed to reforming Islamic law and education, but these young nationalists were less interested in religion. They did not hesitate to use ideas from Europe. They campaigned for the creation of European-style political, legal, and educational institutions. Among the institutions they hoped to create in the Islamic world were parliamentary systems and secular universities.

Devout Muslims, and especially the ulama, received these ideas with skepticism. They were angry that the nationalists seemed to have set aside their commitment to Islam. Most of the nationalists felt that religion should be left out of politics. They

■ *Kemal Ataturk, ruler of Turkey from 1923 to 1938, meets with Rida Shah Pahlavi, who ruled Iran from 1923 to 1941. Both men emerged from the ranks of the military to seize power over their respective nations. Admirers of European-style political institutions, both men attempted to create secular societies in which Islam was kept out of political and economic life. The Ayatollah Khomeini would later overthrow Rida Shah's son, Muhammad Rida, in the 1979 revolution in Iran.*

were not against religious practices and beliefs, but they felt that these had no place in the fight for independence.

As the 20th century progressed, European rule over the Islamic world gave way to independent states. In 1923 Turkey—which was one of the few areas in the Islamic world never to have fallen under European rule—was declared an independent republic. The leader of the Turkish nationalist movement, Mustafa Kemal Ataturk (d.1938), immediately set out to make Turkey a fully secularized state. The Shari'ah was replaced by a European-style code of law; Muslim dress and customs were banned. Today, Turkey remains the most secularized country of the Islamic world. In 1993, Tansu Ciller, leader of the True Path Party, became Turkey's prime minister, making her the second Muslim woman to be elected head of state, after Benazir Bhutto in Pakistan. Today, Turkey continues to strive for a balance between the political forces of secularism and Islam.

Independence soon followed for other regions in the Islamic world: Iraq in 1932; Syria in 1947; Indonesia in 1950; Egypt in 1952; Morocco, Tunisia, and the Sudan in 1956;

Malaysia in 1957; Nigeria in 1960; and, following a long and costly revolution, Algeria in 1962.

Pakistan came into being in 1947 in the midst of India's fight for independence from England. An Islamic nationalist movement in India, called the Muslim League, had won support among the Muslims of India for a separate Muslim state. The League was finally able to create the state of Pakistan, but only after a long civil war with India in which hundreds of thousands of Muslims and Hindus lost their lives. In 1971, the eastern half of Pakistan broke away after a bloody civil war to become Bangladesh.

The Struggle for Power

In the majority of the newly independent Muslim states, political power was held by secular governments. Many were controlled by military officers with no interest in combining religion and politics. This set the stage for conflict between the secular nationalists and the various groups within their states that supported Islamic forms of government. For these groups, it was time to return to Islamic principles and the rule of the Shari'ah.

■ *Tansu Ciller was Prime Minister of Turkey from 1993 to 1996. Leader of Turkey's influential True Path Party, she has also served the Turkish government as economics minister.*

Two such groups were the Society of Muslim Brothers, founded in Egypt in 1929 by Hasan al-Banna, and the Jamaat-i-Islami, founded in India in 1941 by Mawlana Mawdudi. For both al-Banna and Mawdudi, Islamic society was under attack not only by the European colonial powers, but also by the secular nationalist movements. They savagely criticized these movements for adopting Western ideas and for abandoning Islam. For both leaders, the separation of religion and politics was a violation of Islamic principles. They argued that Islam brought together all aspects of life, including politics and religion.

Mawdudi, al-Banna, and others like them won the support of large numbers of Muslims. Unlike many of the ulama, they were dedicated to political activity. Their commitment to the faith struck a chord in the minds and hearts of many Muslims over the first half of the 20th century.

The support these groups enjoyed did not escape the attention of the political leaders of the Islamic nations. Often, their first reaction was to clamp down on these Islamic movements, sending their leaders to prison. Eventually, however, some leaders of Muslim states began to take a different approach. They tried to use religion to win the support of the broad population. In Egypt, the government of Gamal Abd al-Nasir (d. 1970) sponsored a religious newspaper and called for the support of the ulama of the Al-Azhar mosque. Al-Nasir's successor, Anwar Sadat (d. 1980), went even further in associating his government with religious symbols, events and institutions such as al-Azhar. In Syria, Hafiz al-Asad (d. 2000), who seized power there in 1970, repeatedly used Islam in this way in the 1970s and 1980s. These gestures toward Islam, however, did little to change the unpopularity of their governments. By the late 1960s, from Indonesia to the Middle East, clear signs of discontent with government policies were apparent. Many of these governments called themselves democratic or representative, but the opposite was usually true. Their leaders ruled with little popular support. These governments were also responsible for poor economic policies and rampant corruption. There were growing social problems, among them high rates of poverty and crime. To many devout Muslims, the obvious reason for these problems was the decline of Islamic values and practices.

A New Commitment to Islam

In the late 1960s and early 1970s, as political, social, and economic problems continued to grow, Muslims throughout the Islamic world began to renew their commitment to Islam. There was a growing sense that Muslims should look to their own traditions and use them to revitalize their societies. Some now began to share the opinion that Islam—and particularly the Shari'ah—contained all the guidance needed by individuals and society.

The new dedication to Islam took different forms. Many ordinary Muslims made a greater commitment to the beliefs and practices of Islam, and many began to lead what was seen as a more Islamic lifestyle. This included studying the Koran; carrying out daily prayer and the fast of Ramadan faithfully; supporting institutions such as clinics, schools, and youth centers run by religious organizations; and adopting modest styles of dress and public behavior. In cities and towns throughout the Islamic world, it became more common to see young women wearing plain, long dresses and scarves over their hair.

However, for many Muslims, the commitment to Islam was more than a return to Islamic ways. It was a call to political action. Across the Islamic world, young Muslim men and women joined or formed political movements. Their message was that the time had come to put an end to secularized, Western-style governments and to make the Shari'ah the foundation of Islamic society.

The Islamic Revolution

Probably no single event in the mid-twentieth century had as much impact on the minds of Muslims as the 1979 Islamic revolution in Iran. The revolution was carried out by a broad coalition made up of ulama, student groups, leftist organizations, and others—and was supported by a large number of ordinary Iranians. Its goal was the overthrow of Shah Muhammad Reza Pahlavi (d. 1980).

The voice of the revolutionary movement was Ayatollah Khomeini (d. 1989), a religious scholar. Khomeini had harshly criticized the shah's policies as being contrary to the teachings of Islam. Many Iranians were drawn to Khomeini's powerful religious message. He attacked the shah for undermining Islam with secularism and for his assault on the powers of the ulama. For his criticism, Khomeini was arrested and sent into exile.

From exile, Khomeini called for the overthrow of the shah and the creation of an Islamic style government headed by the ulama. He argued that because the ulama were trained in Islamic law and theology, they were the only ones who could properly lead an Islamic government and society. In fall of 1978, revolution broke out and in early 1979 the shah fled the country. Khomeini returned in that year to Tehran and became the spiritual head of the Islamic Republic.

The effect of the revolution on the rest of the Islamic world was electric. For the first time, an Islamic movement had successfully opposed a modern secular government. For many Muslims—particularly the new activists—the Islamic Revolution was enormously encouraging. It was a sign that a return to the ideals of Islam and the duties of the Shari'ah could bring success. It also confirmed what Muslims could accomplish through political action.

The initial burst of enthusiasm for Khomeini and the Islamic Revolution gradually died away. The majority Sunni world did not fully accept Khomeini, a Shi'i leader, so relations with other Muslim countries suffered. Moreover, the new Islamic government of Iran soon became as undemocratic as the shah's government had been. People who had grown accustomed to secular freedoms chafed under strict Islamic rule. Music was banned, women were forced to wear the *burqa* (a garment covering the face and body), and other freedoms were strictly curtailed.

By the mid-1990s, Iran was suffering under economic hardships. People began to call for more progressive economic policies. In 1998, Iranians elected a moderate president, Mohammed Khatami. The outcome was a victory for the many women and young people who had voted for reform, rejecting conservative policies such as the dress code and other restrictive regulations.

In the spirit of reform, Iran appointed its first female senior judge, and freedom of speech improved. Muslim authorities lifted the ban on women leading congregational prayers for other women, which had been a problem in all-girl schools. Iran's more moderate government took steps toward improving relations with Europe and the United States, and saw its relationships with other Muslim countries improve as well. The struggle between conservative hard-liners and reformers has continued, however. But for many Muslims, the Islamic Republic has proved that a government modeled on strict Islamic principles can succeed and prosper.

The Balkan Crisis

At about the same time as the Islamic revolution in Iran, in Eastern Europe a rise in Serb nationalism proved disastrous for Muslims in the former Yugoslavia. After the death of the Communist leader Josip Broz Tito (d.1980), the ethnic groups that had made up Yugoslavia began to break apart along nationalist lines: Serb, Croat, and Muslim. The strongest of these were the Serbs, with dreams of a "Greater Serbia," which would reunite all of the lands that had historically been Serbian. Although they were concentrated in Bosnia, Muslims were not a majority in any of the areas where they lived. They had always tried to live peacefully beside their neighbors. Now they found themselves caught in the midst of a war not of their making.

In March 1994, Muslims and Croats in Bosnia signed an agreement that created Bosnia and Herzegovina as an independent state. This did not assure their safety, however. In spite of United Nations peacekeeping efforts, in July 1995 the Serb army attacked Srebrenica, a Muslim "safe area." They took the Muslim men to a field outside the town and shot them. Srebrenica thus became the site of the worst massacre of civilians in Europe since World War II. Exactly how many Muslim men died may never be known, but the numbers were horrific. The event brought a new phrase into the English language: "ethnic cleansing."

The Dayton Peace Accords of 1995 ended the war, but not the hatred. Thousands of Muslims were left homeless, unable to return to towns where hostility still runs high. In addition, many Muslim homes were seized by Serbs or burned to prevent their owners from reclaiming them. The massacre also left thousands of widows and fatherless children, whose only offense was to be Muslim.

Bosnia is not the only region in which Muslims suffered tremendous losses. When Yugoslavia was breaking up, Kosovo, a region of Serbia that was originally part of Albania, wanted its independence. Here, too, the people were predominantly Muslim. Serbia sent troops into Kosovo to put down revolutionary activity. Waves of refugees fled to neighboring countries. In 1998, Serbian troops killed many of the civilian inhabitants of Drenica, mostly Muslim women and children. Since then, a campaign of ethnic cleansing has continued in the northern part of Kosovo.

Afghanistan: The Taliban

After the break-up of the Soviet Union in 1992, former Soviet countries such as Afghanistan, Azerbaijan, Turkmenistan, Uzbekistan, and Tajikistan, previously secular and Communist, have emerged with growing Islamic identities. Only in Afghanistan, however, has there been a move toward a purely Islamic state.

Afghanistan had been engaged for years in civil war, with many groups vying for power. Muslim on Muslim violence had claimed many victims. In 1994, a new group, made up mostly of Afghani religious students, burst onto the world scene. They called themselves the Taliban. They announced that their mission was to free Afghanistan from its corrupt leadership and to create a society in accord with Islam. A strong and well-trained fighting force, they lost no time in taking control.

In the towns they occupied, the Taliban issued decrees to the public. They required men to wear turbans and beards, and to pray five times a day, in the mosque if possible. Women were ordered to wear the burqa. They were told that under Islam, their role was to be wives and the mothers of the next generation, and so they were forbidden to work outside the home. The Taliban also banned education for girls until religious scholars could draw up an appropriate curriculum, an activity that would have to wait until the Taliban had taken control of the entire country.

By 1998, the Taliban had come close to its goal of unifying Afghanistan under its rule. But its heavy-handed interpretation of Islamic law created new problems. The ban on women's employment fell with unequal force on widows and their children—barred from working, female heads of households faced starvation. The UN strongly criticized the Taliban's restrictions on education, health care, and employment, and suspended aid.

The Taliban's activities in the name of Islam have brought censure from more moderate Islamic countries. Only Pakistan, Saudi Arabia, and the United Arab Emirates recognize the Taliban government; all other Islamic nations and the UN recognize the previous government. Many mainstream Muslims find the Taliban's treatment of women anti-Islamic. They point out that Muhammad's first wife, Khadijah, was a widow and a merchant, and her role in the religion is honored.

The Middle East

The establishment of Israel as a nation in 1948 left Palestinian Arabs without a homeland. Muslim Arabs were displaced from a land they had inhabited for centuries. Their plight was largely unnoticed by the Western powers until the 1967-war between Israel and the Arab states of Egypt, Syria, and Jordan. In a few short days, the three Arab armies met defeat. In the process, Jerusalem—the third holiest city in Islam—fell into Israeli hands.

Over the next twenty years, relations among countries in the Middle East stabilized somewhat. The Palestinians, however, still suffered under repressive Israeli rule, watching Israeli settlers claim lands that had been theirs. Beginning in 1987, the Palestinians began to assert themselves politically in what was called the "Uprising," or *Intifada*, under Yassar Arafat. Continued acts of resistance have legitimized the Palestinian cause and eventually brought the Israelis and the Palestinians to the bargaining table.

Many unresolved issues remain between Israel and the Palestinians. One is Jerusalem, the location of the al-Aqsa Mosque, from which the Prophet ascended to heaven. Devout Muslims call for its liberation from Israel, as well as for a separate Palestinian state.

Islam in America

Islam is the fastest-growing religion in America. In the mid-1970s, 800,000 people, or .4 percent of the American population, identified themselves as Muslims. In the mid-1990s, the number had swelled to 3,560,000, and by mid-2000, to over four million, or 1.4 percent. These numbers include people born into the religion, immigrants to America who have brought their Islamic

■ *An open area beside the Prophet's Mosque in Medina. A Muslim couple, he an Indian and she an American, walks with their young daughter. Most Muslims living and working in the United States today are immigrants or descendants of immigrants from Muslim nations. Increasing numbers of Americans, however, are converting to Islam.*

beliefs with them, and converts, who may be Caucasian, African American, Hispanic, and even Native American.

A growing group among the Muslims of America is the Nation of Islam. An American movement now under the leadership of Louis Farrakhan, it has more than 1,600,000 followers. Mainstream Muslims generally say that the Nation is not part of the Islamic community. They find many of the Nation's teachings, particularly those about other races and religions, to be out of step with traditional Islam, which recognizes all people and all races to be equal before God. In recent years, however, the Nation has shown signs of change in ways that may bring it more into line with orthodox Islam.

The Islamic community exercises increasing influence in American life. One area in which Muslim influence may be seen is in education. American Muslims have long emphasized the importance of educating young people in the ethics and beliefs of Islam, so as to equip them to lead morally responsible lives. To Muslims, this emphasis on moral responsibility is important for two reasons: first, to offer a clear alternative to Muslim young people in American society, and second, to demonstrate to Americans at large the stress Muslims place on living morally and ethically.

Thanks to a greater awareness of Muslims as a presence in America, Muslim students enrolled at American colleges and universities such as Syracuse and Harvard may now find themselves able to observe dietary laws. They may also choose secondary education from the Islamic perspective. The American Islamic College, established in Chicago in 1983, is a fully accredited four-year college offering courses in sciences, computer sciences, economics, history, and other disciplines, as well as Arabic and Islamic studies. In 1996, the School of Islamic and Social Sciences, the first Muslim school for graduate studies, opened in Leesburg, Virginia.

Islam Facing the Twenty-First Century

As the Islamic world moves into the 21st century, it looks back on three centuries of struggle. Beginning in the 18th century, Muslim culture lost much of its vitality, as its political and economic power gave way to Europe's greater technological and military might. Europe's march through the Islamic world continued through the 19th and early 20th centuries. During that time Islamic thinkers tried to understand the reasons for Europe's dominance and to find ways for Islam to adapt to the new ideas that were entering the culture from the West. In the end, their soul-searching gave rise to a nationalism that blended the religious and legal culture of Islam with notions of independence and enabled them to throw off European dominance. Today, the Islamic world holds a stronger position in the world at large than at any time since the 18th century.

Increasingly, Muslims today are young. Many have grown up in a secular world. As they look around them, they see a society full of problems — including unemployment, crime, and declining moral values. Like generations of young people before them, they are looking for new approaches, new ways to order their lives in a difficult world. Islam is one such way. Always renewing itself, it offers them a real alternative for change. The force of the Islamic revival sweeping the world today is the force of youth, with its belief that the world can become a better place.

Islam is, by its very nature, an endless revolution, an eternal quest to reach out to God. Muslims are committed to challenge what they see as wrong. They may not be passive. Whatever happens, the future of Islam will include a great deal of debate and perhaps even conflict. Although activism seems on the rise, most in the Islamic world oppose militancy and extremism, or feel that the Shari'ah should not be the basis of government. It seems most likely that Islam will remain a religion and civilization that encompasses a variety of points of view. This was true of Islam early in its history, and it remains true today.

■ A section from the 10th chapter, or surah, of the Koran. This is a plain but elegant example of Arabic script. The passage speaks of the certainty of God's judgment and warns sinners that they will be condemned by God if they persist in their evil actions.

GLOSSARY

Adhan—The call to prayer made five times daily from the minarets of mosques

Allah—The Islamic term derived from Arabic and meaning God

Ayah—A verse of the Koran. Each chapter (see surah) contains one or more of these verbs

Barakah—Spiritual blessing. Used to refer to the powers of particularly religious individuals, such as "saints"

Burqa—A garment covering the face and body

Caliph—Term deriving from the Arabic term *khalifah*. It was the title used by the rulers of the Islamic Empire. It can also mean representative or deputy

Dhikr—"Remembrance" of God. Used by the Sufis to refer to their ritual practices

Eid al-Adha—The annual feast day of sacrifice held on the tenth day of the Islamic month Dhu al-Hijjah, the month of pilgrimage

Eid al-Fitr—The annual festival in which the end of the month of fasting, Ramadan, is celebrated

Ghazwah—"Raid" in pre-Islamic period and in early Islam

Hadith—The collection of reports or a single report relating the words and deeds of the Prophet Muhammad. The words and deeds themselves are known as the Sunnah, or "way of acting"

Hajj—Pilgrimage, specifically to Mecca. The annual pilgrimage is held in the month of Dhu al-Hijjah and is one of the Five Pillars of Islam

Hijrah—"Emigration." The term used to refer to the journey by the Prophet Muhammad and his companions from Mecca to Medina in 622

Ihram—The white garments worn by pilgrims in Mecca during the annual pilgrimage (see *hajj*). These garments are also indicative of ritual purity

Imam—Used by Muslims to refer to the leader of a session of prayer or a religious teacher. The Shi'ah use the term for special individuals viewed as the religious and political leaders of the community

Islam—An Arabic word meaning to submit or surrender, specifically to the will of God

Jami'—The congregational mosque used particularly, though not only, on Fridays for the weekly sermon and noon prayer

Jihad—"Striving" for one's religion. Often translated as "holy war"

Khutbah—The sermon given, usually by a prominent religious figure, in the congregational mosque at the Friday noon prayer session

Kuttab—Koranic school usually attended prior to the start of regular schooling

Mahdi—The messianic figure who, it is believed, will arrive at the end of time to bring justice and order to the world

Masjid—A local or neighborhood mosque (see *jami'*)

Mawlid—The festival commemorating the birthday of a religious figure, usually a "saint." Another term used is *musim*

Mu'adhdhin—Or muezzin. The individual who makes the call to prayer (see *adhan*) five times daily from the minaret of a mosque

Muslim—A believer of Islam; anything pertaining to the religion, law, or culture of Islam

Niyyah—"Intention" necessary for the proper completion of a ritual, such as prayer

Qadi—Judge, usually appointed by the state

Qiblah—The direction of Mecca in which all Muslims must pray. In mosques it is indicated by the *mihrab*, or prayer niche, found in every mosque

Sadaqah—Voluntary almsgiving

Salat—Prayer. One of the Five Pillars of Islam

Sawm—Fasting, particularly the annual fast of Ramadan. One of the Five Pillars of Islam

Shahadah—"Bearing witness" to the oneness of God and to the prophethood of Muhammad. Also one of the Five Pillars of Islam

Shari'ah—The system of law in Islam based on the Koran and Muhammad's Sunnah. Often translated as "holy law"

Shaykh—Elderly man, teacher, or tribal leader. Also the head of a Sufi organization or center

Shirk—Associating any object or being with God. The one unforgivable sin of Islam

Surah—A chapter of the Koran

Tafsir—Interpretation, usually of the Koran

Tariqah—A Sufi order

Tawah—Ritual circling of the Ka'bah in Mecca that is part of the annual pilgrimage for Muslims

Ta'ziyah—Passion play held each year in Shi'i communities to commemorate the death of Husyan ibn Ali

Ulama—Religious and legal experts

Ummah—Community, specifically a religious community. Most often used in Islam to refer to the Islamic community

Wudu'—Ritual cleansing performed before each session of prayer

Zakat—Legal almsgiving considered obligatory for Muslims, and calculated on the basis of income. One of the Five Pillars of Islam

FOR FURTHER READING

Aziz, Zahid. *Introduction to Islam.* Columbus, Ohio: Ahmadiyya Anjuman Isha'at Islam Lahore, Inc., 1993.

Banks, William H., Jr. *The Black Muslims.* Philadelphia, Pa.: Chelsea House, 1997.

Dunn, John. *The Spread of Islam.* San Diego, Calif.: Lucent Books, 1996.

Irwin, Robert. *Islamic Art in Context.* New York: Harry N. Abrams, Inc., 1997.

Matar, N.I. *Islam for Beginners.* New York: Writers and Readers Publishing, Inc., 1992.

Nasr, Seyyed Hossein. *A Young Muslim's Guide to the Modern World.* Chicago: Kazi Publications, Inc., 1994.

Shah, Indries. *Seeker After Truth.* London: Octagon Press, 1992.

Swisher, Clarice, ed. *The Spread of Islam.* San Diego, Calif.: Greenhaven Press, 1998.

Weiss, Walter M. Islam: *An Illustrated Historical Overview.* Hauppauge, N.Y.: Barron's, 2000.

Wormser, Richard. *American Islam: Growing Up Muslim in America.* New York: Walker Publishing Company, 1994.

INDEX

Abbas I 40
Abbasid Dynasty 35–39, 57
Abd al-Nasir, Gamal 103, 116
Abduh, Muhammad 112, 113
Abu al-Abbas 35
Abu Bakr 21, 28, 30, 33
Abu Hanifa 55, 57
Abu Sufyan 26
Abu Talib 12, 18, 21
al-Adawiyyah, Rabia 70
al-Afghani, Jamal al-Din 112
Afghanistan 120
Ahmad ibn Hanbal 57
Alid Family 32, 34, 58–60, 85
Ali ibn Abi Talib 31–32, 58, 62, 63, 98
Ali Zayn al-Abidin 60, 62
Almsgiving (*zakat*) 79–80; (*sadaqah*) 80
Arabian Nights 35
Arabian tribal life 14–16, 28, 30
Arafat/Mount of Mercy 81
Arafat, Yassar 121
al-Asad, Hafiz 62, 116
Ashura 83, 85
al-Askari, Hasan 63
Association with God (*shirk*) 47
Ataturk, Mustafa Kemal 114
Ayatollah Khomeini 62, 117–118
al-Ayyubi, Salah al-Din (Saladin) 37–38
al-Azhar mosque and university 37, 92, 93

al-Badawi, Ahmad 97–98
Badr 23–24
al-Banna, Hasan 116
Banu Hashim 12
Banu Thaqif 20
al-Basri, Hasan 70
Battle of the Trench 25
Bearing witness (*shahadah*) 77–78
Bhutto, Benazir 114
Birthday festivals (*mawlid/musim*) 96–98
Bosnia 119
Burqa 118, 120
Buwayhid Dynasty 37
Byzantium/Byzantine Empire 18, 30, 39, 46–47

Caliph 28, 30, 31, 32, 33, 34, 35, 36, 37, 38, 39, 42
Call to prayer (*adhan*) 76
Childhood 44, 98–100
Christians/Christianity 8, 9, 10, 11, 16, 17, 18, 19, 20, 36, 38, 42, 47, 55, 58, 71, 74
Ciller, Tansu 114, 115
Circling the Ka'bah (*tawaf*) 81
Circumcision 100
Clitoridectomy 100
Crusades 9, 38

Day of Judgment 65
Death/funeral rites 102–103
Direction of prayer (*qiblah*) 92–93
Divine revelation 10, 49, 57
Dome of the Rock 38
Druze sect 61

Euphrates River 36
European colonialism, 110–112

Farewell Pilgrimage 27
Farsi language 90
Fasting (*sawm*) 78–79
Fatimid Dynasty 37, 61
Feast of Fastbreaking (*Eid al-Fitr*) 95
Feast of Sacrifice (*Eid al-Adha*) 96
Five Pillars of Islam 74–82
Food/drink 102
Friday sermon (*khutbah*) 91–92

Hadith 52–54, 55, 57, 90, 92
Hanafi legal school 55
Hanbali legal school 57
Hasan ibn Ali 33, 62, 63, 98
Heaven 21, 38, 48–50
Hell 48–50
Hijaz 16
Hulagu 38
Husayn ibn Ali 33–34, 57, 58, 59, 60, 62, 63, 82–85, 98

Ibn Abd al-Wahhab 107–108
Imam 58–60, 61, 62–66, 84, 85, 97
Imam 61, 77, 83, 91, 102, 103
Intention (*niyyah*) 74
Iqbal, Muhammad 112, 113

Isfahan 39, 40, 41
Islamic calendar 22, 27
Islamic community (*ummah*) 11, 22, 25, 27, 31–32, 50, 52–54, 57, 58, 69, 106
Islamic education 36, 37, 42, 51, 87, 99, 100
Islamic Empire 30, 32, 34, 35, 36, 37, 38, 39, 41, 42, 53, 54, 55
Islamic legal system/schools of law 36, 50, 54–57
Islamic Revolution (1979) 62, 117–118
Isma'il ibn Ja'far 61
Israel 61, 121

Ja'firi legal school 57
Jamaat-i-Islami 116
Jerusalem 21, 23, 30, 38, 121
Jesus 10, 20, 21, 47
Jewish scripture/Torah 10, 46
Jews/Judaism 11, 20, 23–25, 36, 47, 50, 58, 70
al-Jilani, Abd al-Qadir 72
Journey to Medina (*Hijrah*) 20–22
Judge (*qadi*) 36

Ka'bah 16, 17, 21, 26, 80, 82
Karbala 33, 60
Khadijah 18, 19, 22, 99
Khan, Sayyid Ahmad 112
Kharijites 31–32, 34–35
Khatami, Mohanned 118
Khaybar 25
Khurasan 35
Koran 8, 10, 11, 27, 36, 43, 44–52, 54–56, 69, 79, 90, 91, 99–103, 123
Koranic chapter (*surah*) 46
Koranic interpretation (*tafsir*) 51–52
Koranic recitation 44, 46
Koranic school (*kuttab*) 100
Koranic verse (*ayah*) 46
Kosovo 119
Kufah 33, 55, 60

al-Mahdi 65
Malik ibn Anas 55
Maliki legal school 55, 56
al-Mansur 35, 57

Marriage 100–101
Martel, Charles 34
Mawdudi, Mawlana 116
Meccan society and leadership
16–18, 20–27
Mehmet II 39
Mina 81
Minaret (*ma'dhanah*) 76
Misconceptions about Islam, 8–9
Mongols 38, 39, 104
Moses 10, 20, 21, 46
Mosque 22, 76, 77, 86, 92–93, 94,
95, 99
Mosque, congregational (*jami'*)
92–93
Mosque, local (*masjid*) 92
Mosque of Ibn Tulun 93
Mu'awiyah 31, 32, 33
Muezzin (*mu'adhdhin*) 76
Mughal Empire 39–40, 42, 104,
108
Muhammad ibn Abd Allah (the
Prophet) 10, 12, 16–27, 28, 30,
31, 32, 36, 38, 39, 43, 44, 45, 46,
47, 48, 49, 50, 52–54, 62, 63, 65,
66, 69, 76, 82, 95, 96, 98
Muhammad ibn al-Hanfiyyah 60
Muhammad ibn Isma'il 61
Muhammad's miraculous journey
21, 38
Muharram 33–34, 83
Mulay Idris 97–98
Muslim Brotherhood 114
Muslim League 114
al-Musta'sim 38
al-Muwatta 55–56

Naqshibandiyah Sufi order 108
Nationalism 113–114
Nusayri (Alawi) sect 61–62

Oneness of God 20, 26, 47
Ottoman Empire 39–42, 104, 110

Pahlavi Dynasty 68
Pahlavi, Reza Khan 68
Palestine 56, 140
Persia 37, 38
Pilgrimage (*hajj*) 17, 80–82
Pilgrimage garment (*ihram*) 80

Pilgrimage guide (*mutawwif*) 80
Polygyny 101
Prayer (*salat*) 74–78, 91–92
Prayer niche (*mihrab*) 92
Prophets/prophethood 10, 46, 47

Qadiriyah Sufi order 72
Qajar Dynasty 68

Raids/raiding (*ghazwah*) 14–15, 23
Ramadan 78–79, 94, 95, 117
Ramadan meal (*iftar*) 95
Recital (*rawda-khani*) 85
Reform movements 106, 107–108,
112–113
Religious scholars (*ulama*) 41, 106,
107, 112, 113, 114, 118
Remembrance (*dhikr*) 85–86, 95
Rida, Rashid 112
Risalah 56
Ritual washing (*wudu'*) 76, 92

al-Sadat, Anwar 116
al-Sadiq, Ja'far 57, 61, 62
Safavid Empire 39–40, 41–42, 68,
72, 104
Saints/saint worship 86–87
Samarra 36, 63
al-Sanusi, Muhammad ibn Ali
109
Sanusiyah Sufi order 109
Sasanian Empire 30–31
Satan (*Iblis*) 49–50
Sa'ud tribe 87
al-Sadhili, Ahmad ibn Abd Allah
72–73
Shadhiliyah Sufi order 72–73
al-Shafi'i, Muhammad ibn Idris
56–57
Shafi'i legal school 56–57
Shah of Iran 117
Shah Wali Allah 108–109
Shari'ah 11, 36, 54–55, 66, 106, 112,
113, 115, 117, 118, 123
Shi'i Muslims/Shi'ism 6–7, 32–34,
37, 57, 58–69, 71, 118
Spirits (*jinn*) 16, 20, 49
Spiritual blessing (*barakah*) 86–87,
98
Standing cermony (*wukuf*) 81

Striving (*jihad*) 109
Sufis/Sufism 70–73, 85–87, 106
Sufi centers 71, 73, 86
Sufi masters (*shaykh*) 71
Sufi orders (*tariqah*) 72
Suhraward 72
al-Suhrawardi, Umar ibn Abd
Allah 72
Suhrawardiyah Sufi order 72
Sunni Muslims/Sunnism 6, 33,
37, 58, 63, 65–66, 118
Surat al-Fatihah 48, 100, 103

al-Tabari, Abu Ja'far Muhammad
ibn Jarir 51–52
Ta'if 20
Taj Mahal 39–40
Taliban 120
Tanta 97
al-Thaqafi, Mukhtar 60
Tito, Josip Broz 119
Tomb visitation 86, 87
Tribal leader (*shaykh*) 9–10, 14–15
True Path Party 114, 115
Twelfth Imam (The Hidden
Imam) 63–65, 66
Twelve Imams 62–65
Twelver Shi'ah 8, 62–65, 67–69
Twelver Shi'i (*ulama*) 67–69

Ubayd Allah 61
Uhud 24
Umar ibn al-Khattab 30, 33, 124
Umayyad Dynasty 30–35, 58, 60,
61
Urdu language 90
Uthman don Fodio 108–109
Uthman ibn AffanWahabbi move-
ment 107–108

Yathrib 17, 21
Yazid ibn Mu'awiyah 33
Yemen 8, 61

Zaydi sect 60–61